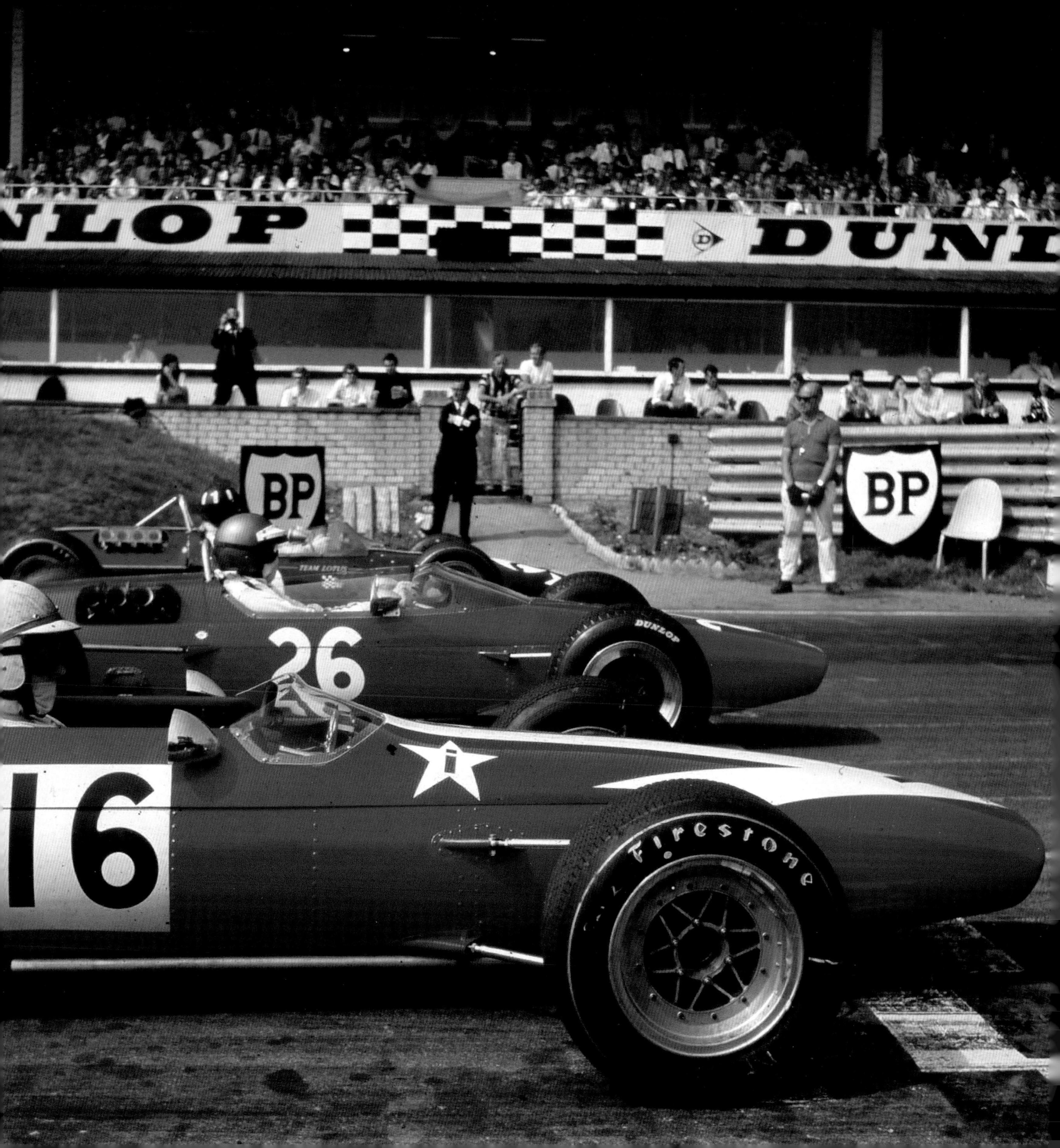
NLOP
DUNL
BP
BP
TEAM LOTUS
26
DUNLOP
16
Firestone

The Classic
MOTOR RACING CIRCUITS
OF EUROPE

DAVID VENABLES

David Venables
Formerly the Official Solicitor, David Venables is the Assistant Editor of the Vintage Sports Car Club Bulletin and a regular contributor to *The Automobile*. He is the author of motor racing histories on 1930s *Voiturette* racing Napier, Bugatti and Alfa Romeo and also the *Official Centenary History of Brooklands*. His most recent books are *British Racing Green* and *French Racing Blue*. He lives in Sussex and is a keen vintage motorist, driving a 1930 Aston Martin and a 1936 Fiat.

Ludvigsen Library
All this book's illustrations are from the collection of the Ludvigsen Library or have been sourced for the book by the Library. Much in demand from publishers, editors, authors, enthusiasts, restorers and collectors, the Library's holdings include some 150,000 original negatives and more than 50,000 original transparencies. Print and digital files include some 100,000 images in addition to those held in negative form for a total approaching half a million images.

Available in the Library are high-quality images of Formula and sports-car racing, works visits, car tests, motor shows, personalities and domestic transport. Included are celebrated collections from the work of Rodolfo Mailander, Stanley Rosenthall, Max Le Grand, Cyril Posthumus, John Dugdale, Edward Eves and Ove Nielsen, also including the photography of Karl Ludvigsen. Early prints and glass negatives portray racing and motoring throughout the 20th Century. The Library website is **www.ludvigsen.com**

The Classic Motor Racing Circuits of Europe
David Venables

First published 2010

ISBN 978 0 7110 3481 5

Published by Ian Allan Publishing
an imprint of Ian Allan Publishing Ltd. Hersham, Surrey, KT12 4RG
Printed in England by Ian Allan Publishing Ltd. Hersham, Surrey, KT12 4RG

Visit the Ian Allan Publishing website at:
www.ianallanpublishing.com

Produced by Chevron Publishing Limited
Project Editors: Chevron Publishing and Karl Ludvigsen
Cover and book design: Mark Nelson
© Text: David Venables
© Circuit diagrams: Donna Askem

Chevron Publishing would like to acknowledge the kind assistance of Karl Ludvigsen and the Ludvigsen Library in the preparation of this book.

Ian Allan
PUBLISHING

CONTENTS

Preface

PREFACE

THOUGH libraries of books have been written about racing drivers, the cars and their exploits in competition, relatively little has been recorded about the tracks and circuits, the theatres where the dramas have been played out.

Europe's earliest racing was over open roads from city to city. This heroic and hazardous form of racing ended with the tragedies of the aborted Paris-Madrid race in 1903. Closed-circuit racing took its place, often with circuits of great length. In parallel with this development came the first purpose-built tracks, epitomised by Brooklands.

After World War 1 the classic circuits began to emerge and with these came more purpose-built tracks such as Montlhéry and Monza. The classic road circuits, at first formed from country roads, grew and developed with better surfaces, eased corners and permanent pits and grandstands.

After World War 2 the classic road circuits continued to develop. The stimulus was the desire for greater speed, so these gradually lost their resemblance to their original incarnation. Silverstone, a primitive wartime bomber airfield, gradually evolved into a circuit of classic status.

Huge changes came in the 1960s and 1970s with the realisation that circuits needed to be safer for both drivers and spectators. Also opposition grew from local communities, which found the inconvenience of closing public roads unacceptable. Some of the classics were abandoned while others were changed to a point where little of the original character or even the features remained.

A new force entered motor racing: the power of television. Producers and sponsors wanted shorter tracks on which logo-liveried cars were continuously in front of the cameras. The technical problems of TV production were eased by shorter circuits. This brought a fundamental change. Developers and circuit owners realised that purpose-built circuits ensured a maximum number of paying customers. New bespoke venues emerged in the latter decades of the 20th century.

This trend has evolved further, to the point where some of the newest circuits seem to place more emphasis on the quality of the ancillary facilities than the track itself. This has resulted in a new generation of short and convoluted tracks on which overtaking is difficult.

Perhaps contests on these new circuits are lacking the drama which was such an essential part of those staged on the heroic courses of the past. I hope that this book will ensure that those circuits — scenes of such marvellous races — are not forgotten.

David Venables
January 2010

CHAPTER 1

Le Mans

Arthur Duray passes through Connerré village in his Lorraine-Dietrich during the 1906 French Grand Prix. The track is well barricaded.

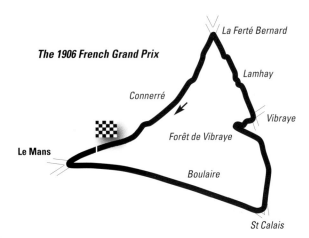

The 1906 French Grand Prix

Le Mans
La Ferté Bernard
Lamhay
Connerré
Vibraye
Forêt de Vibraye
Boulaire
St Calais

L E MANS. Perhaps the most stirring words in motor racing, evoking legendary battles between cars and drivers, racing through the night, headlights ablaze. Remembered as well are great triumphs and tragedies.

It all began in the earliest days of motor racing. After the turn of the 20th Century the Gordon Bennett Trophy was an annual competition for three-car national teams. The cars and every component used, right down to tyre valves, had to be made in the country of origin.

As motor racing burgeoned, French manufacturers chafed at the limitation of a Gordon Bennett team to a mere three cars. The rest of the nation's many car makers had no chance of glory. Bowing to pressure, the *Automobile Club de France* (ACF) decided that in 1906 it would hold a Grand Prix that was open to all manufacturers. The Gordon Bennett was abandoned. For the inaugural French Grand Prix a huge 64-mile (103km) circuit was chosen to the east of the city of Le Mans in western France. It was a rough, undulating triangle with the start and finish adjacent to a hairpin on the city's outskirts.

The Grand Prix was a success. It was held over two days, 26 and 27 June, with competitors covering six laps each day. Thirty-two starters battled over roads which were rough despite tar-sealing and rolling. At the end of the second day, to huge French delight, the winner was a Renault, driven by Hungarian Ferenc Szisz. He was greatly helped by a new-fangled device, the detachable wheel rim. This let him change his shredded tyres in a fraction of the time taken by his opponents.

In 1907 the Grand Prix moved to Dieppe. However the new format didn't work out quite as French manufacturers intended. The Grand Prix became a success story for Italian and German cars with French teams merely playing walk-on parts. As there was no French glory in it, after 1908 the Grand Prix was abandoned for four years.

The local *Automobile Club de la Sarthe* realised that there was still a need for a major race, so in 1911 it organised the Grand Prix de France as a stand-in event. A new 33.75-mile (54km) circuit started at Pontlieu on the southern outskirts of Le Mans. It ran across country returning to the start on what later became the famous Mulsanne straight. The race was a success, including one of the first for Bugatti when a tiny 1.3-litre Type 13 driven by Ernest Friderich came second.

The ACF ran the official Grand Prix again in 1912 at Dieppe but the *AC de la Sarthe* repeated their race at Le Mans in 1912 and 1913. Its fields were almost of full Grand Prix quality with additional classes for voiturettes and cyclecars. Then came World War 1. Racing did not resume in an exhausted, war-shattered France until 1920. That August the Coupe des *Voiturettes* was held on a 10-mile (17km) circuit which ran from Pontlieu down the Mulsanne straight, then across country to Arnage and back to Pontlieu. It drew a big field which was dominated by the Bugatti team.

In 1921 the ACF was ready to run the full French Grand Prix again. It returned to Le Mans with a 10.6-mile (17km) road circuit which was later to become the basis of the legendary 24-hour course. The surface was poor with broken patches and flying stones. Once again French pride was dented as victory went to an American Duesenberg driven by Jimmy Murphy.

The *AC de la Sarthe*, which had become the AC de l'Ouest (ACO), made an imaginative and epoch-making decision in

1923. It organised a 24-hour race for sports and touring cars to encourage the development of road cars and especially their electrical and lighting systems. The ACO returned to the 1921 circuit, which was a stern test because little had been done to improve its road surfaces. To assist weak headlamps the corners were illuminated by army searchlights and acetylene lamps. The crowd was entertained by a fair with a jazz band and a cinema behind the rudimentary pits.

The early part of the 1923 race was run in heavy rain. Despite this only three of the 33 starters retired and it became a fierce battle between a team of Chenard-Walckers and a Bentley. One of the French cars won, averaging 57.16mph (92.06km/h). For the 1924 race attempts were made to improve the surface, the funfair was expanded and large car parks were built. This accompanied the first of the legendary Bentley wins. There was a big step forward in 1926 when permanent pits were built, replacing the provisional tarpaulin and scaffolding. Work continued on the surface of the track and three types of surfacing were used.

From the very first 24-hour race the major corners at Mulsanne and Arnage had been lined with sandbanks to prevent cars running amok. Many desperate scenes resulted as drivers tried to dig their errant cars out of the banks with illegal shovels, smuggled over the fence to them by team members.

The 1927 race established the first of countless Le Mans legends. The three-car Bentley team and several others were in a multi-car collision at White House Corner soon after dusk. Pulled out of the melee, one Bentley carried on with bent axle and frame and broken headlamps, driven by motoring writer

The start of the 1920 Coupe des Voiturettes sees Baccioli in No 12, a member of the winning Bugatti team. No 11 is Violet in a Major and No 13 is Dumoulin with a Tic-Tac.

Sammy Davis and Harley Street specialist Dudley Benjafield, the least-glamorous pairing of the legendary 'Bentley Boys'. They went on to a glorious and improbable victory.

Three more Bentley victories followed. Little had been done to the circuit, but in 1929 came the first major change. The Pontlieu hairpin on the outskirts of Le Mans was lopped off, reducing the lap distance to 10.1 miles (16.3km). The 1930 race, in which Bentley defeated Mercedes-Benz, saw the first women competitors in the 24 Hours, driving a Bugatti. They finished and won the 1.5-litre class.

With Bentley bankrupt, French hopes were high in 1931. Bugatti, financed by tyre-supplier Michelin, prepared a team for the 24 Hours. Alas, the tyres were inadequate. One of the Bugattis left the road on the Mulsanne straight, killing a spectator. During 1931 the ACO bought approximately 185 acres (75 hectares) of land which included the pits and grandstand area and extended as far as the Mulsanne straight.

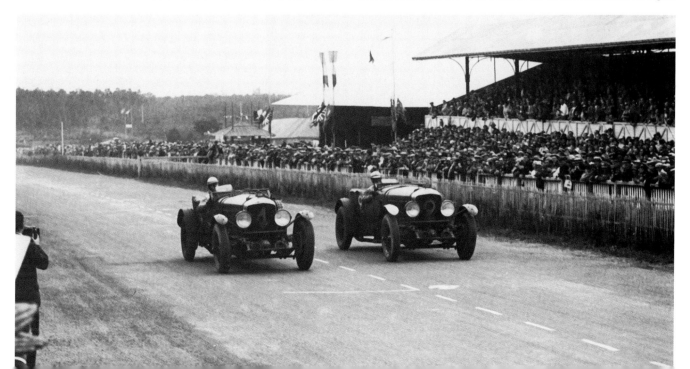

Glen Kidston and Woolf Barnato parade past the pits in their Speed Six Bentleys after winning the 1930 24 Hours. This was the last race in which the Bentley team participated.

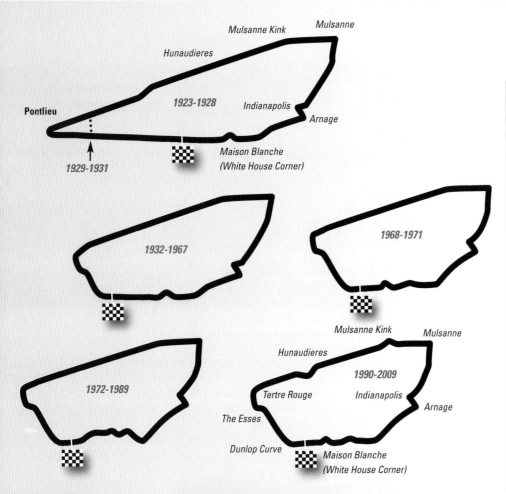

The development of the Le Mans circuit from 1923 to 2009.

1931: a Caban and a Lorraine race on the section of track which runs into the outskirts of Le Mans. This was abandoned after the 1932 race.

On this a new road was built including a series of bends which became known as 'The Esses'. The road joined the Mulsanne straight at a new corner, Tertre Rouge, and was lined with earth banks and palisades. This reduced the lap distance to 8.4 miles (13.5km) for the 1932 race.

The circuit was now much in the format it would retain until 1956. New permanent grandstands were built facing the pits. The pits were improved, each being fitted with an automatic refuelling system. To entertain less-enthusiastic spectators a nine-hole golf course was made on the infield.

A run of four Alfa Romeo wins was ended by a Lagonda success in 1935. This was a surprise as Lagonda was bankrupt and the receiver funded the cars. There was no race in 1936, when France was hit by a wave of industrial unrest, but the three races before World War 2 saw a huge restoration of French pride with two Bugatti wins bracketing a Delahaye success.

There was some sadness in 1937. Another White House multi-crash saw two drivers dead. The postscript was poignant too. Robert Benoist, co-driver of the winning Bugatti, would become an SOE hero during the war and be hanged by the Nazis in 1944.

When the German Army rolled across France after the Dunkirk evacuation, the remaining British forces retreated towards the French Atlantic ports. Among them was 'Mort' Morris-Goodall who had raced Aston Martins at Le Mans. He recalled later that despite the retreat he found time to do a lap of the circuit in an army lorry.

The ground behind the grandstands had become an airfield. For a few short days, before France fell and the German occupation began, it was the base of two RAF Hurricane squadrons. The airfield then became the home of a Messerschmitt Bf 110 unit which took part in the Battle of Britain. The Luftwaffe extended the airfield and demolished the pits. The airfield was bombed frequently during the 'softening-up' of German defences before D-Day. Sammy Davis, the 1927 victor, found a scene of desolation and destruction when he visited in August of 1944.

The ACO started from scratch, rebuilding their circuit and facilities. It hoped to run the 24-Hours in 1947, but the restoration took two years and normality only returned in 1949. The circuit was repaired with its pits, stands and facilities rebuilt. Before the race the circuit

In the immediate post-war years the Le Mans 24 Hours draws a mixed field. In the 1951 race a works DB2 Aston Martin leads a diminutive 750cc Crosley Special into Arnage Corner.

was formally reopened by the French President, Vincent Auriol.

The first post-war race saw a Ferrari victory, the first of nine wins in the following years. It was followed by a Lago-Talbot winning for France in 1950, then came the first Jaguar success in 1951. After World War 2 German teams were not welcome in France, but in 1952 Mercedes-Benz made a comeback. The race was led until the 22nd hour by a Lago-Talbot driven single-handed by Pierre Levegh, but with two hours to go its engine broke and the Mercedes swept home to a 1-2 win. Speeds were rising and in 1953 an American Cunningham was timed on the Mulsanne straight at 154mph (249km/h). Jaguars, which had won in 1953, bowed to Ferrari in 1954 after a bitter struggle in the rain.

The 1955 24 Hours promised to be an heroic race with Ferrari, Jaguar and Mercedes-Benz teams in intense combat with the world's greatest drivers. The opening laps saw a titanic struggle. Then after two and a half hours of racing the Mercedes 300SLR of Pierre Levegh collided with the Austin Healey of Lance Macklin and was catapulted into the crowd in front of the main stands. Levegh and 81 spectators were killed. The race continued although the Mercedes team was withdrawn. It was a hollow win for Jaguar.

The 300SL Mercedes-Benz coupés head the line-up for the run-and-jump start of the 1952 race. The narrowness of the track was a factor in the 1955 disaster.

The start of the ill-fated 1955 24-Hours. Luigi Musso leads in a 300S Maserati, from the 750 Monza Ferrari of Dreyfus. No 26 is the Austin-Healey of Lance Macklin followed by No 20 the 300SLR Mercedes-Benz of Pierre Levegh. This pair would be involved in the terrible accident two hours later.

After this, motor racing's greatest single tragedy, there was talk of a permanent ban on racing in France, but pragmatism prevailed. The sport resumed after important decisions on safety. The ACO realised that its circuit needed changes. It was too narrow for the 170+mph (270km/h) the cars were reaching. The line of the pit straight was changed and the track was widened. The changes reduced the length of the lap

11

Umberto Maglioli's 121LM Ferrari passes a Frazer Nash at the beginning of the Mulsanne Straight in the early stages of the 1955 race. The days of Armco barriers are yet to come.

Top right: The D-type Jaguar after its victory at Le Mans in 1955. Mike Hawthorn is on the left of the car, his co-driver Ivor Bueb is on the right with his back to the camera. It is a subdued celebration following the appalling crash which killed 82 spectators.

Far right: Olivier Gendebien, sharing the 1958 win with Phil Hill, takes his 250 TR Ferrari onto the Mulsanne Straight in the early evening.

by 30 metres. For 1956 the number of starters was reduced from 60 to 55. The race saw another Jaguar win, repeated in 1957.

The revised circuit remained unchanged until 1968. Meanwhile Ferrari domination began. It was broken in 1959, when after 31 years of striving for success, an Aston Martin won. Then it all changed in 1966. The most renowned race of all, Le Mans was followed world-wide. America's Ford realised the huge publicity benefits a win could bring. Application of massive resources produced a Ford win in 1966, repeated in 1967, 1968 and 1969. Speeds were still rising, so to temper the pace of the cars past the pits a chicane was built in 1968 between White House Corner and the pits.

In 1967 the French Grand Prix returned to Le Mans after an interval of 46 years. It ran on the new Bugatti circuit which used the pit straight, then turned right at the Esses on a convoluted 'Mickey Mouse' course through the car parks before returning to the main track. The drivers disliked it and the crowds stayed away. The Grand Prix didn't return, but the Bugatti circuit is still used for the 24-hour Motorcycle Grand Prix.

In 1970 a piece of the great Le Mans tradition went. The famous Le Mans start, in which drivers dashed across the track to their cars, was abandoned. Drivers sat in their cars in front of their pits to wait for the flag. Other changes came a

HENRI PESCAROLO

HENRI PESCAROLO has an unique record. Not only a four-time winner of the Le Mans 24-Hour race, he has also made a remarkable 33 appearances in the race.

Born in 1942, son of a Paris surgeon, Pescarolo abandoned medical studies in 1964 after showing promise in a competition organised by the magazine *Sport Auto* to find new French driving talent. In 1965 he joined the Matra F3 team, taking the European F3 title in 1967. When Matra moved up to F2, Pescarolo responded by taking the runner-up title in the 1968 F2 championship.

Pescarolo found little success with Matra when the French team entered F1, achieving a solitary podium with third at Monaco in 1970 when he was 12th in the World Championship. It was the same story with subsequent moves to Williams, March, BRM and Surtees.

The narrative was different with Matra's sports-racing cars. No French car had won at Le Mans since 1950. Throwing huge resources into the quest, Matra sought a prestigious victory. Pescarolo took part in abortive efforts in 1966 — his first 24-Hours drive — 1967 and 1968. To huge national pride a win came in 1972 when Pescarolo shared the car with British double World Champion Graham Hill.

Henri was back on the Le Mans winners' rostrum again in 1973 and made it a Matra hat-trick in 1974 when he co-drove to a notable nine World Sports Car Championship rounds. He had become a national hero whom France honoured with appointment to the Legion d'Honneur.

After Matra pulled out of racing Pescarolo's talents remained in demand. Recognised as the top sports-car driver, he went to Alfa Romeo and thence to Porsche. After an interlude with the French Rondeau-Ford, in 1984 came the fourth Le Mans win at the wheel of a Porsche. The Sports Car Championship wins continued to accumulate. Pescarolo drove for the German-Swiss Sauber-Mercedes team and for British Jaguar and Spice. His last major win came in 1991 with a Porsche in the Daytona 24 Hours.

'Pesca' continued to compete in the 1990s. Fittingly his last race drive was at Le Mans in 1999, when he finished ninth. Though he hung up his helmet, Pescarolo's involvement with the sport continued. He formed Pescarolo Sport in 2000, building sports-racers. His cars have continued to be a force in sports-car racing, race wins and places still being notched up. A Pescarolo won the Le Mans Endurance Championship in 2006 and 2007. Both the man and his cars have an honoured place in French motor racing.

year later when a rolling start was introduced and three drivers were permitted to take the wheel.

The Porsche era had begun, but missile-maker Matra rescued French pride with a hat-trick of victories in 1972, 1973 and 1974. Renault also sought Le Mans glory, hurling in massive resources, but had to wait until 1978 for a deserved win. In parallel there had been more changes to the circuit. In 1972 a new 1.8-mile (3.0km) section replaced the old track between Arnage corner and the 1968 chicane. This bypassed the notorious White House corner.

The year 1980 saw another historic first. The Ford-powered French Rondeau was co-driven to victory by its constructor Jean Rondeau. After that it was seven years of Porsche domination. Meanwhile the line of the Tertre Rouge Corner had been changed to accommodate the new Paris-Rennes Autoroute. This was followed by alterations to Mulsanne Corner where a roundabout was sited for a new industrial estate.

In the month of June Le Mans is an annual semi-religious pilgrimage for 50,000 British fans. They had something to cheer

*Far left: **Carroll Shelby powers the winning Aston Martin DBR1/300 through Mulsanne Corner during the 1959 race***

The 917LH Porsche, taking second place in 1970, has an eye-catching 'psychedelic' paint scheme.

Fitted with fins, the 1971 version of Porsche's 917K had an engine enlarged from 4.5 to 5.0 litres. This one won Le Mans for Helmut Marko and Gijs van Lennep.

Gaining its reward for so much investment and dedication, the Renault-Alpine A442B takes the flag in the 1978 race.

in 1988 when Jaguar returned in triumph. The Union flags waved for Jaguar again in 1991.

Inevitably speeds kept rising. In 1988 a Peugeot-powered WM hit 253mph (409km/h) on the Mulsanne straight. The ACO knew this was a recipe for disaster, so in 1990 the Mulsanne straight was interrupted by two chicanes that put paid to such extreme speeds in the future. More work was done on the pit area before the 1991 race, separating the pit road from the main track. Since 1991 the circuit has been altered little with only slight changes to corners in the Dunlop Bridge section after the pits.

Peugeot found its share of Le Mans glory in 1992 and 1993. Japanese cars were appearing in increasing numbers, lured by the reputation of the great race. A Mazda win, with its trademark rotary engine, was the reward in 1991. Another run of Porsche wins was broken by the British McLaren in 1995. BMW also waved the German flag in 1999.

Then Audi, bearing the four-ring symbol that had taken Auto Union to Grand Prix glory between the wars, came to Le Mans. A first win in 2000 was followed by two more. For all British enthusiasts 2003 had a deep symbolism; the green Bentleys returned and won. Perhaps delight was mildly tempered by the knowledge that now Bentley was Audi-owned.

After this brief resurgence of the green, Audi came back. It broke new ground with a hat trick of wins with diesel-engined cars from 2006. Sharing the Audi glory was Dane Tom Kristensen, who scored a record eight wins between 1997 and 2008. To French relief, Peugeot took the honours in 2009 aided by a diesel and KERS, the regenerative braking system also used in Formula 1.

Le Mans has seen motor racing for over 100 years. The *Circuit Permanente de la Sarthe* and its legendary 24-hour race are a magnet for enthusiasts the world over. More than 250,000 spectators throng there annually for what most regard as the greatest motor race on the most historic and evocative circuit of all.

Davy Jones, Raoul Boesel
and Michel Ferte bring this
Jaguar XJR-12 into second
place in the 1991 24 Hour
race.

The victorious Audi crosses
the line at the end of the 2008
race, winning by a margin of
only four and a half minutes.

CHAPTER 2

Targa Florio:
The Madonie circuits

Vincenzo Florio
at a Targa event
in 1920.

Count Giulio Masetti
crosses the line to win the
1922 Targa Florio in a 1914
Grand Prix Fiat.

Alfred Neubauer, later the
legendary Mercedes team
manager, competes in the
1922 Targa with this
Austro-Daimler 'Sascha'.
He finishes 19th and wins
his class.

VINCENZO FLORIO was a young man who had everything. He was the younger son of Ignazio Florio who played a major role in dragging medieval Sicily nearer the edges of the modern world. Ignazio's interests were wide, making him a rich man. Vincenzo was born in 1883, but as a younger son had little to do with his family's business affairs, which were entrusted to his elder brother. When Vincenzo was 14, Ignazio's death left the boy with funds to indulge his fancies. Not the typical playboy, he was fascinated by mechanical things, especially the rapidly developing motor car.

Vincenzo bought various cars. With a Panhard he competed in two sprint meetings at Padua in the autumn of 1902, winning both. He entered for the Paris-Madrid in 1903 but his elder brother stepped in and stopped the venture. Despite family disapproval he continued to race, driving Darracqs and Mercedes.

In 1904, inspired by James Gordon Bennett and his eponymous trophy, Florio instituted the *Coppa Florio*. This was a two-lap race held over a tough, dusty 116-mile (186km) circuit at Brescia. Florio drove in his own race, finishing

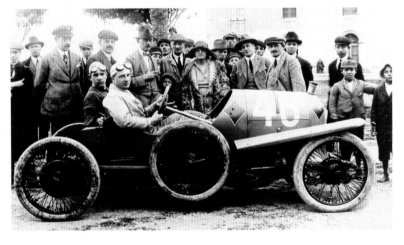

third. It was held again in 1906, when he came ninth in a Mercedes. The *Coppa Florio* series continued into the 1920s.

Florio moved up a class when he drove a Mercedes in the 1906 French Grand Prix at Le Mans, but he had already launched one of the all-time legendary races. Florio wanted a race in his home island. Sicily's roads were primitive, however, and only really suited to horse-drawn traffic. Nevertheless Vincenzo chose a 90-mile (144km) circuit which started on the north coast at Cerda, 30 miles (45km) east of Palermo. It climbed a tortuous path up into the mountains, twisting and turning. Passing through small, primitive villages, it reached 3,670ft (1,118m) then plunged its writhing path down to sea level again. At first called the Madonie circuit, the original 1906 course later became known as the Great Madonie.

The first Targa Florio was held in May 1906. Its field of 10 started at 10-minute intervals, covering three laps of the circuit. There were six finishers. Victory went to Alessandro Cagno in an Itala, after 9 hours 33 minutes' racing. He was the first recipient of the magnificent gold Targa, made by a Paris goldsmith. He was lucky as the Itala's crown wheel stripped as he crossed the finish line.

Word got around about this amazing new contest. In 1907 it drew 50 entrants and 46 starters. It was an international field with factory teams from France and Germany. The winner was Fiat-mounted Felice Nazzaro, who divided his time between looking after Florio's stable of cars and

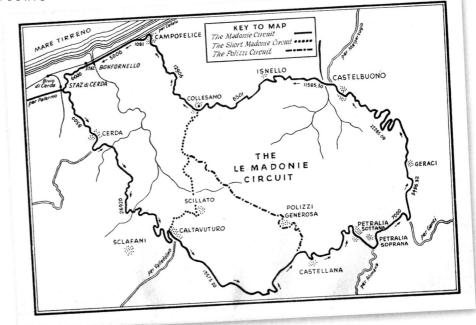

testing Fiats. He was chased home by another famous name, Vincenzo Lancia. Then a Fiat driver, he would soon break away to start his own car manufacture. Despite the testing course there were 30 finishers. The race was an enthralling spectacle for the Sicilians, who lined the course, cheering on the competitors.

The next Targa was a bit of a let-down with only 13 starters but it was closely fought. Lancia lost out when his tyres failed. Victory in 1908 went to Vincenzo Trucco with an Isotta-Fraschini. In 1909 there was a major earthquake at Messina, but Florio decided the race should go ahead, though it was reduced to a single lap. The race saw the first appearance of one of Lancia's own machines. Florio himself drove a Fiat to make up the thin entry, coming second behind an SPA.

From 1908 until 1912 the major makers had signed a pact to demur from racing. This hit the Targa Florio entry lists. Only eight cars set out in the 1910 race, three of which were the bizarre Lion-Peugeots with 2.8-litre twin-cylinder engines nearly three feet high. They looked odd but scooped the pool, taking the first three places.

Normally unbelievably tough, in 1911 the course was even worse as the race was run in torrential rain. The cars struggled through thick mud. A new and significant marque appeared, ALFA from Milan, soon to become one of the all-time racing greats. After 1911 there was a change. Perhaps with the expectation of a larger entry, the race was run as the *Giro di Sicilia*, around the whole island, a single lap of 652 miles (1,042km).

Although Italy did not enter World War 1 until May 1915, all motor racing stopped when the rest of Europe began battling in August 1914. When the war ended racing didn't resume at once. A war-torn and exhausted continent needed over a year to recover its breath. Vincenzo Florio was the first to start again. Run in November 1919, his Targa Florio was Europe's first post-war race. It was an unpropitious time of year with gales, rain, snow flurries and mud everywhere.

Perhaps appreciating that a more gentle course was needed, Florio chose a new circuit, the Medium Madonie. After its climb into the mountains it cut out a part of the Great Madonie course when returning to the coast. The lap was reduced to 61.1 miles (108km). In the entry of 24 were names that would soon become famous: Antonio Ascari, Giuseppe Campari and Enzo Ferrari.

The 1919 race was a battle between the French Ballots and Peugeots with the Italian cars outpaced. At the end of the fourth and last lap André Boillot in a Peugeot lost control, crashing into a grandstand only a few yards from the finish line. He reversed over the finish to be told that was illegal, so drove

The Targa Florio, showing all three circuit variations: the short Madonie Circuit, the Polizzi Circuit (medium Madonie Circuit) and the main Madonie Circuit.

On his way to his legendary 1930 win, Achille Varzi doesn't stop when his P2 Alfa Romeo catches fire. His mechanic Tabacchi beats out the flames with a seat cushion.

back to the scene of his crash, turned round and crossed the line again to win.

In 1920 it was mud and more mud. The race was won by a Nazzaro, Felice having gone into the manufacturing business, with Enzo Ferrari second in an Alfa Romeo. After World War 1 Florio was more welcoming than other race promoters to German entries. The 1921 Targa Florio enjoyed a factory entry of a Mercedes driven by Max Sailer, a 28/95 model with a 7.2-litre engine. After early rain the sun shined on a fierce fight between Sailer and Giulio Masetti in a 1914 GP Fiat, the Italian getting the honours by just two minutes, a wafer-thin margin in the Targa.

Masetti was back in 1922, now a member of the Mercedes team and driving one of the legendary 1914 GP cars. Jules Goux led until the last lap in a Ballot, but his brakes were failing, his tyres were worn out and his radiator was leaking.

More drama followed in 1923. Antonio Ascari's Alfa Romeo led on the last lap, then stopped almost within sight of the line with a mechanical problem. He restarted with two helpers hanging onto the car as it completed the short run to the line. Outraged officials insisted he went back to the place where he had stopped to do the run to the line again without the helpers. While Ascari obliged, his team-mate Ugo Sivocci swept past and won, leaving Antonio in second place.

Despite economic chaos and runaway inflation in Germany, Mercedes kept racing and took a team of blown 2.0-litre cars to the 1924 Targa. Christian Werner had a lucky win for Mercedes when Ascari's luck ran out again. He was leading as he took the last corner, but his Alfa's engine seized.

Tazio Nuvolari leaves the start of the 1931 Targa in his 8C2300 Alfa Romeo. The mudguards make a major contribution to his win, protecting him from the mud bath ahead.

Masetti moved up and won again by a two-minute margin from Jules Goux. Among the drivers was another name which would become a legend in the next decade, Alfred Neubauer, driving an Austro-Daimler Sascha.

Ascari pushed it across the line but meanwhile Werner had taken the race.

In 1925 the Bugatti era began. Until 1924 the Grand Prix Bugattis had been ugly ducklings, but then the Type 35

ACHILLE VARZI

In a race famous for its heroic drives, Achille Varzi scored one of the greatest Targa Florio wins in 1930. Born in 1904, the son of a rich textile manufacturer, Varzi began racing motorcycles in 1923. After winning two-wheel Italian Championships he moved into cars in 1927. He raced with Bugattis and then Alfa Romeos.

After a string of wins in 1929 and the Italian Championship, Achille Varzi was signed up by the Alfa Romeo team in 1930. Unlike most of his fellow Italian drivers, Varzi was quiet, elegant and introverted.

Racing against his bitter rival Tazio Nuvolari, in the 1930 Targa Florio Varzi led from the start. After three laps the spare wheel in the tail of his P2 Alfa broke away, damaging the fuel tank. With his tank leaking, at the start of his fifth and last lap Varzi realised he could run out of fuel. He made a stop at a refuelling depot in the mountains where his mechanic Tabacchi grabbed an extra can.

On the long straight beside the sea running to the finish, the Alfa's engine stammered. It was out of fuel. Varzi didn't stop. Tabacchi climbed onto the tail

and poured the contents of the can into the tank. Some splashed on the exhaust and caught fire. While Varzi raced flat out, Tabacchi beat out the flames with a seat cushion so the pair could arrive first at the finish to victorious acclamation.

It was a different story in 1931 when the Madonie course was a rain-swept mudbath. At the start of the last lap Varzi still led in a Bugatti, but the mud overwhelmed him and he dropped to third behind the hated Nuvolari.

Their rivalry culminated at Monaco in 1933 when they duelled for 99 of the 100 laps and Varzi won when Nuvolari's engine burst on the 100th lap. When the German teams entered Grand Prix racing in 1934, Varzi went to Auto Union.

Achille Varzi's career suffered after he was introduced to drugs by the wife of another driver; addiction followed. He was 'clean' after Word War 2 and drove for Alfa Romeo again. A member of the all-conquering Tipo 158 team, he gained both wins and places.

In practice for the 1948 Swiss GP at Berne Varzi's Alfa overturned. He died in the arms of his rival, Louis Chiron, a few minutes later. The racing world mourned the ice-cold, quiet, calculating Varzi, who had been one of the top three drivers of the early 1930s.

Stirling Moss makes a pit stop in the battered 300SLR Mercedes during the 1955 Targa Florio and prepares to hand over the car to Peter Collins. The pair go on to win.

Luigi Musso shares the winning drive in the 1958 Targa with Olivier Gendebien in this 250TR Ferrari. It is Musso's last win. He is killed in the French GP seven weeks later.

appeared, one of the most beautiful racing cars of all time. Not only did it look right, the performance lived up to the looks. In 1925 Meo Costantini, Bugatti's racing manager, ran away with the Targa in a Type 35 and repeated the win in 1926, leading home a Bugatti 1-2-3.

The Medium Madonie circuit became a Bugatti fiefdom. Materassi won in 1927 with Albert Divo taking the race for Bugatti in 1928 and 1929. In 1928 history was made as the race was led for four laps by the Czech woman driver Elisabeth Junek, her Bugatti painted in black and yellow instead of the usual blue. When on the fifth and last lap she slowed with a leaking water pump, Divo went through to win. The delay dropped her to fifth place. For 1930 Alfa Romeo revamped its all-conquering 1924/5 P2 GP car. This took Achille Varzi to an amazing win.

Bitter antipathy between Varzi and Tazio Nuvolari went back to a 1928 dispute in which Varzi alleged that Nuvolari had ripped him off over car preparation. In 1931 the Targa went back to the awesome Big Madonie. Varzi had moved to Bugatti while Nuvolari had a new 8C 2.3-litre Alfa Romeo. Varzi led for

two laps in a Type 51 Bugatti — then it rained. The road turned to mud. Nuvolari, whose Alfa had front mudguards, pulled ahead as Varzi found it hard to see the road through rain and flying mud. At the end Nuvolari won with Varzi third, eight minutes behind. In the evening, after the race, Vincenzo Florio saw Nuvolari outside his hotel in Palermo. Congratulating him on the win, he received the terse reply: 'I'm glad I beat Varzi!'

In 1932 a new circuit the Short or Piccolo Madonie was instituted. Halfway into the mountains on the outward leg of the Big course, a new road funded by Benito Mussolini cut across country to rejoin the return leg. This reduced the lap distance to 44.7 miles (72km). The course was still narrow and precipitous but the surface was improved.

Perhaps some of the original magic left the Targa in the 1930s. It gradually became a virtual Italian national race with few foreign entries. It was run for Grand Prix cars until 1935, then in 1936 it became a mere two laps for sports cars. Worse was to come. Between 1938 and 1940 the mountainous Madonie was abandoned. The Targa was run as a 1,500cc voiturette race in a park in Palermo.

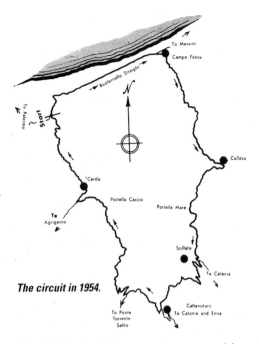

The circuit in 1954.

The 1961 Targa is the first victory for the Ferrari 246SP driven by Olivier Gendebien and Wolfgang von Trips.

Vincenzo resumed his Targa Florio in 1948 as a sports-car event, but until 1950 he ran it as a round-Sicily race. In 1951 it came back to the Piccolo course with the only British victory in the long history of the race. Franco Cortese scored an unexpected win with a 2.0-litre Frazer Nash. For the next three years it became a battleground for the Italian teams with fierce fights between Ferrari, Lancia and Maserati.

In 1955 the Targa Florio assumed a new significance as it was the last round of the World Sports Car Championship. The title lay between Ferrari and Mercedes-Benz, Ferrari leading by 19 points to 16. One 300SLR of the Mercedes team was driven by a British pair, Stirling Moss and Peter Collins. They went off the road several times in the rain, denting the car extensively. 'Despite our efforts to write the machine off', as Collins put it, they came home to win, followed by another 300SLR driven by Juan-Manuel Fangio and Karl Kling. This gave Mercedes the Championship by a single point and marked the last time the company raced for over 30 years.

After a lull the Targa was a Championship round again in 1958. This time it was a Ferrari-Porsche fight with the red cars coming out on top. This started a rivalry which ran for over a decade with shared honours until the mid-1960s when Porsche established dominance.

Though no longer a race which attracted the top Grand Prix drivers, the Targa was a magnet for the leading sports-car drivers. To drive in it became an ambition for a host of amateur racers. The treacherous mountain roads, lined with cheering spectators in the villages, were irresistible. In 1972 Alfa Romeo again scored with a T33, driven by local man Nino Vacarella who had shown a unique talent for the notorious course.

By the early 1970s the testing Madonie course was no longer acceptable to the manufacturers competing for the World Sports Car Championship. It was so unlike the circuits on which the other rounds were contested that after 1973 it was dropped from the series. The last major race went to Porsche.

Thereafter the Targa ran until 1977 as a virtual national race. Time had moved on, making it no longer practicable to run such a vast event, so a magnificent part of motor-racing history ended. Despite the extraordinary dangers of the course, during its long history only one spectator and two drivers had been killed. Vincenzo Florio died in 1959, creator of a magnificent race that inspired countless heroic legends.

Ferrari's new rear-engined designs worked yet again. This Ferrari 246SP driven by Willy Mairesse, Pedro Rodriguez and Olivier Gendebien won the 1962 Targa Florio.

Paolo Gargano and Ludovico Denza finish in 24th place with their Alfa Romeo Giulia TZ in 1965.

This Alpine-Renault A110, driven by Jacques Feret and Pierre Orsini in the 1964 race, is typical of the multitude of private entrants attracted to the Targa.

Swiss Jo Siffert and Briton Brian Redman win the 1970 Targa with this Porsche 908. Crowds jamming the roadsides were always a daunting feature.

CHAPTER 3

Brooklands

S. F. Edge's team of Napiers line up before the start of the 24-hour record run in 1907.

IN 1905 Hugh Locke-King, a rich landowner with a large farming estate at Weybridge about 20 miles (30km) south-west of London, drove to Italy to watch the Coppa Florio. There were no British entries. When he asked why, Locke-King was told that there was nowhere in England where cars could be tested and prepared for racing. He returned home determined to build a track on his estate. He sought the advice of S. F. Edge and Charles Jarrott, then the leading British racing drivers. Both had won major races in Europe, Edge the victor in the 1902 Gordon Bennett Trophy.

Locke-King wanted a wide track with long sweeping curves so consulted a military engineer, Henry Holden, who said immediately that if the track were to accommodate cars at high speeds, the curves must be banked. Holden designed a 2¾-mile (4.42km) track that filled the available site, specifying steeply banked curves at the north and south ends, the Members' and Byfleet bankings.

Locke-King had sold a piece of land adjoining the site, so instead of both bankings being linked by straights, the eastern link had a slight reverse curve. From this a diagonal section of track led across the infield to join the northern banking. Called the Finishing Straight, it was designed as the finishing point for races. The River Wey ran across the site so Holden's design had two bridges crossing the river. One was a complicated structure carrying a section of the banking.

Work on the track began in January 1907. A huge cutting was made through a hill at the northern end, taking the track through the hillside. Using largely manual labour, with some 2,000 men employed, the track was completed by July 1907. Its surface was concrete, which was then at the forefront of advanced building technology. Locke-King had underestimated the cost so the venture nearly bankrupted him.

The Brooklands Automobile Racing Club (BARC) was formed to organise racing. Before the first meeting in July 1907, S. F. Edge booked the track for an attempt on the World 24-Hour record using a team of three Napiers. His aim was to average over 60mph (96km/h). The run was a success. A new record was set, but it seems that the concrete had not cured fully. The track was damaged, bringing problems in the future.

The BARC copied many aspects of racing at Brooklands from horse racing, including distinctive colours for the drivers. Throughout Brooklands' active life, the majority of races were handicaps. Locke-King's aim that the track should be used for testing and development was realised immediately. It also became the venue for record attempts.

Motorcycle races went into the programme in 1908, when a famous match race was held between a Fiat and a Napier which had formerly held the Land Speed Record. After the

Right: A social scene in the paddock at the opening meeting of 1907 finds S. F. Edge in a black cap, with his daughters, while Charles Jarrott, his great rival and a leading driver of the day, looks at a Napier entered by Edge.

Napier broke down the Fiat won, credited with a lap record of 121.64mph (195.71km/h); a figure which was subsequently thought suspect. Fatal crashes in the first two seasons brought much unfavourable publicity.

The first long-distance contest in England was held in 1911 with a 100-lap race for standard production cars. The race was run again in 1912, won by a Singer by the close margin of 0.8 second. The track was being used regularly for records up to 13 hours' duration. History was made in February 1913 when Percy Lambert in a Talbot became the first man to cover 100 miles (161km) in the hour. Sadly, in an attempt to improve on his figures Lambert was killed in October 1913. Lambert's ghost is reputed to haunt the track still.

There was more record-breaking history in June 1914. Lydston Granville Hornsted, better known as 'Cupid', brought a 200hp Benz to the track. Running over a measured mile on the Railway Straight, timed over the course in both directions, he set a World Land Speed Record of 124.10mph (199.67km/h). After a shaky start, racing at Brooklands had become successful. The BARC was holding eight or more meetings every season. The 1913 August Bank Holiday meeting had 219 entries.

In 1909 the centre of the site was cleared to make a flying ground. By the end of 1910 it had become the leading centre of British aviation. Many fledgling manufacturers established small factories in the 'Flying Village' alongside the Byfleet Banking. When war came in 1914, flying took a more serious turn. The airfield was used for testing and training pilots while aircraft production took a massive surge.

The biggest manufacturer, Vickers, built a factory adjoining the track at the Fork, the junction of the main track with the Finishing Straight on the reverse curve. This expanded hugely during the war. By the end of the war in November 1918 over 3,000 aircraft had been built at Brooklands. The first flight across the Atlantic was made in June 1919 by a Vickers Vimy, built at the track.

Aircraft production damaged the track extensively so racing couldn't begin again until 1920. That year saw a full season of BARC meetings but no major races. In 1921 a 500-mile (800km) motorcycle race was held. This was a one-off, too shattering for both man and machine to be repeated. A 200-mile race held for 1,500cc cars would become a regular fixture for some years.

The noise of motorcycles aroused the ire of the local residents, who started legal proceedings to have the track closed. It was settled by agreement that cars and motorcycles would be heavily silenced and there would be no night running. Thus was created the unique 'Brooklands silencer' worn by all racers. In May 1922 Algernon Guinness broke the World Land Speed record using the Railway Straight, setting a figure of 133.75mph (215.20km/h) in an 18.2-litre V12 Sunbeam.

Brooklands was establishing a pantheon of local heroes. Foremost among them in the mid-1920s was a Welsh engineer, Parry Thomas. Mostly driving a Leyland-Thomas, a development of a Leyland luxury car which he had designed, Thomas won 33 races, a figure unsurpassed by another driver. He held the lap record several times, setting many World records at the track including the coveted Hour. Brooklands mourned when he was killed in a Land Speed Record attempt at Pendine in Wales in March 1927.

The long-distance races at the track in the 1920s were usually handicaps, held for sports cars. They evolved from a

The 1907 Club House is fully restored by the Brooklands Museum Trust. The red Bentley among the gathering of Bentleys once held the lap record driven by Tim Birkin in 1932.

Brooklands in 1939, the year of its closure.

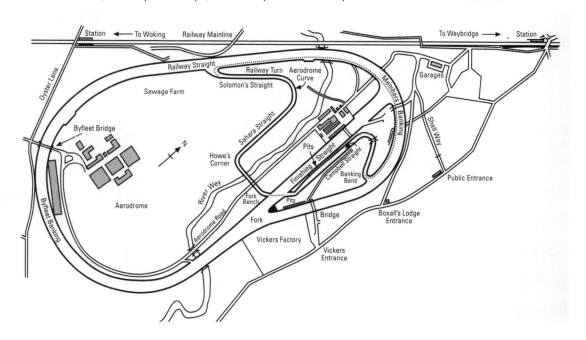

Kenelm Lee Guinness gets off the line with the V12 Sunbeam in 1922 in which he establishes a new World Land Speed record of 133.75mph (215.20km/h).

John Joyce has a lurid moment when breaking the record for the Brooklands Test Hill with an AC in 1923.

The field lines up for the start of the 1925 JCC 200-mile race. The winner was No 11, the Talbot-Darracq of Henry Segrave.

Duel on the banking: John Cobb in the V12 Delage with which he broke the Brooklands lap record in 1929 passes the 2.0-litre GP Sunbeam of E. L. Bouts at the 1930 Whitsun meeting.

Two of the Speed Six Bentleys which dominated the 1930 Double 12-Hour race sweep down the Members' Banking towards Railway Straight.

*The Speed Six Bentley of Barnato and Clement swings onto the Members'
Banking from the Finishing Straight on its way to win the 1930 Double-12.
The inadequate sandbank protects the buses housing the timekeepers.*

*Tim Birkin takes his
26M Maserati round the
Fork while breaking the
Mountain Circuit lap
record in 1931.*

*Holidaymakers have a
good view of the racing
from the River Wey in 1935.*

JOHN COBB

Although tall and powerfully built, John Cobb was a mild, quiet and gentle man. Thus he was, in looks and in the cars he drove, the complete antithesis of his personality. He will always be associated with Brooklands and the huge cars he drove there.

John Cobb was born in 1899. Educated at top British school Eton, he was in the Army at the end of World War 1. By trade a wealthy fur broker, he began racing at Brooklands in 1925 with a 1910 10-litre chain-drive Fiat. One of his early races was in 'Babs', the ill-fated car in which Parry Thomas was later killed attempting the Land Speed Record.

In 1929 Cobb became a major contender at Brooklands with the 10-litre Delage which had held the Land Speed Record in 1924. With the Delage he won major races and took the lap record for the track. In 1933 Cobb commissioned the construction of the Napier-Railton. This 24-litre aero-engined machine was a dual-purpose car, intended to be the ultimate Brooklands racer and to take long-distance World records.

At Brooklands it did all that could be expected. It was the fastest car on the track, twice winning the BRDC '500', at that time the fastest race in the world. In 1935 it took the lap record at 143.44mph (231.69km/h). This was a feat needing great courage. Cobb said afterward, 'It was like seeing how far you could lean out of an eight-storey window without falling.' Never broken, the record stands for all time.

After an abortive attempt at Montlhéry, Cobb took the Napier-Railton to Bonneville's Salt Flats in Utah in 1935. There he took a clutch of 20 world records ranging from one hour at 152.70mph (245.69km/h) to 24 hours at 137.40mph (221.07km/h). Cobb was back in Utah in 1936. Setting new records, he left the hour at 167.69mph (269.81km/h) and the 24 hours at 150.6mph (242.31km/h).

Cobb had greater ambitions. He commissioned the building of a Land Speed Record car designed by Reid Railton, using two 24-litre Napier Lion engines. Taking this to Bonneville in 1938 and 1939, he set a Land Speed Record of 369.75mph (594.92km/h) before World War 2 intervened.

The Railton was back in Utah in 1947, Cobb setting a new record of 394.19mph (634.25km/h) that stood for 16 years. He made one run at 403mph. Like Henry Segrave and Malcolm Campbell before him, Cobb wanted the water-speed record too. A jet-powered boat, Crusader, was built, but broke up in a record attempt on Loch Ness in 1952 after achieving 200mph (320km/h) in one direction. Cobb died in the crash. He was deeply mourned, not only for his achievements but also for his personal qualities.

four-hour race in 1926 to a six-hour contest in 1927 and then, in 1929, into a full 24 hours. The ban on night running required the cars to run for 12 hours, then be locked away for the night, coming out again for another 12 hours the following day. Despite the unusual format, this 'Double-12' was a popular event. It ran for three years, then was replaced by a 1,000-mile sports-car race over two days with 500-mile stints.

In 1929 the British Racing Drivers' Club promoted a 500-mile race which for some years was the fastest long-distance race in the world. It became a regular annual fixture until 1937. In 1926 and 1927 Brooklands was the venue for the British Grand Prix. The 1927 race was the final round of that year's major contests, all of which were won by Delage-mounted Robert Benoist.

The BARC meetings and those run by other clubs continued unabated with over 20 minor meetings during a season, including several evening races. Despite the apparent dangers of racing near the rims of the bankings, Brooklands was a relatively safe track with surprisingly few fatalities over the years. Of the drivers who went 'over the top', several walked away unscathed.

By the early 1930s the limitations of Brooklands were becoming apparent. It had been designed for a maximum lap speed of 120mph (190km/h) but cars were competing which could exceed this by a big margin. The faster cars crowded the top of the bankings, making overtaking hazardous. The plethora of regulations to overcome this earned the track a reputation for fierce officialdom. The ban on night running reduced its value as a record venue.

By the early 1930s Brooklands was becoming a racing backwater. Though still the centre of British racing, it no longer attracted leading foreign drivers. The type of racing, almost all handicapped with titles redolent of horse racing, was far removed from the serious road races held on mainland Europe. Another problem was that the magnificent track was wearing out. It had been built on the cheap, with the concrete laid direct onto sandy subsoil. It had settled and needed constant repair.

Bentleys had been one of the leading marques at Brooklands. The most prominent Bentley driver, who attracted much publicity for his glamour and debonair manner, was 'Tim' (otherwise Sir Henry) Birkin. After Birkin's death from malaria, following the 1933 Tripoli Grand Prix, the acknowledged leading driver at the track was John Cobb. For Cobb, Reid Railton built the Napier-Railton, which had a 24-litre aero engine and was a dual-purpose car intended both for Brooklands and for long-distance records.

From its first appearance in 1933 the Napier-Railton dominated racing on the Outer Circuit, the fast speed bowl.

In 1935 Cobb established an all-time lap record at 143.44mph (231.69km/h). To lap the track at that speed needed immense skill and courage. Cobb went on to break the Land Speed Record in Utah with a Railton-Mobil which was built in workshops at Brooklands, the first car to exceed 400mph (643km/h) in one direction. Cobb was killed when attempting the Water Speed Record in 1952.

In an attempt to bring Brooklands nearer the contemporary racing scene, a number of races were run in the early and mid-1930s using straw-bale chicanes to replicate road circuits. All these were run as handicaps which were hard to follow so lacked spectator interest.

In 1930 the BARC brought in an innovation which had considerable crowd appeal. Short races were run round the 'Mountain Circuit', the course comprising the Members Banking and the linking Finishing Straight. This ran round the public enclosures so overcame the problems of racing on the Outer Circuit which was remote from the spectators. The track still had continuous use for testing and development by the motor industry. Even London buses were seen on test.

When Hugh Locke-King died in 1926 he left all his interest in the track to his widow Dame Ethel. She continued to run the track's managing company. In 1936 she sold all her interests to a new public company. Grandiose schemes were announced for improvements and expansion, but the necessary capital was wanting. The site had great limitations. In an attempt to modernise Brooklands, a new artificial road circuit, the Campbell Circuit, was built and opened in 1937. Running round the edge of the airfield, combined with the banked track, it was a good idea but ten years too late.

It all came to an end in August 1939. The Bank Holiday meeting was the last held at the track before World War 2 intervened. The airfield gained considerable importance when the rearmament programme gathered impetus in the late 1930s. Vickers was making the Wellington, the main RAF bomber for the first three years of the war. The Vickers factory expanded and Hawkers built an assembly line beside the Byfleet banking to produce Hurricane fighters. Most of the Hurricanes that fought in the Battle of Britain were built at Brooklands.

The exigencies of war meant that the track suffered. Workshops and assembly hangars were built on the track and large sections of the banking were removed. At the end of the war it was evident that the track could never be restored for racing so the owners sold it to Vickers in 1946. After that it became a centre of the British aircraft industry. Many famous aircraft including the Viscount and VC-10 were built on the site. This culminated in the manufacture of the largest sections of Concorde.

When aircraft manufacture ended in the 1970s parts of the site became housing and industrial estates, but many sections of the track have been preserved. It is now the home of the very active Brooklands Museum, centred on the old BARC clubhouse. It is used by many motor clubs for meetings, driving tests and even attenuated sprints. With the backing of Mercedes-Benz, which has helped develop the site, the 'Double-Twelve' was revived in 2008 in a new non-speed format.

Hugh Locke-King's original creation was inspired: the world's first purpose-built motor-racing course. Sadly the seeds

John Cobb is push-started in the 24-litre Napier-Railton with which he sets the ultimate Outer-Circuit lap record at 143.44mph (230.79km/h) in 1935.

of its downfall were there at the outset in its proximity to a large urban area and in the inherent limitations of the design. It had glamour and huge excitement, but never fully captured the imagination and support of a wider public. There was always snobbery. Car drivers and lesser motorcycle riders were segregated. The track's slogan, 'The right crowd and no crowding,' said it all.

Throughout its active life Brooklands was of immense value to the British motor industry. Within the confines of the track a specialist community flourished with enormous expertise in the tuning and development of racing machinery. From these roots the present British motor-racing industry, with its worldwide importance, first grew.

During the opening lap of the 1935 Mountain Championship the Fork and Byfleet Banking can be seen in the distance with the paddock on the right.

Brooklands was used continuously for testing. Here an Ulster Aston Martin is put through its paces in 1935 for an Autocar road test. The 1907 Club House can be seen on the left, with the Members' Banking behind.

A group of Bentleys which once raced at the track stand on the restored Members' Banking during a 21st Century reunion.

Lord Howe's T59 Bugatti leaps as it hits the notorious 'bump' on the Members' Banking at the 1936 Whitsun meeting.

This single-seater blower Bentley (left) was used by Tim Birkin (above) on 24 March 1932 to raise the Brooklands Outer-Circuit lap record to 137.96mph, a record which stood for two years before being beaten by John Cobb driving the 24-litre Napier Railton. It is seen here on the restored Members' Banking on a recent outing.

CHAPTER 4

Avus

The NSU team are about to leave the Avus pits before the start of the 1926 German Grand Prix.

KAISER WILHELM II nursed an immense jealousy of Britain. Whatever Britain had, he wanted too: a large navy, an overseas empire. He was also a motoring enthusiast who had supported the 1904 Gordon Bennett Trophy when it was held in Germany, later giving his backing and name to the Kaiserpreis races.

When Brooklands opened in 1907, the Kaiser decreed that Germany must also have a racing and test track. Proposals from many parts of Germany were whittled down to Berlin as a location where the cost of such a facility could best be justified. The *Automobilclub von Deutschland* (AvD) chose a site in the Grunewald forest south-west of Berlin. It would give an imposing route from Berlin to the Kaiser's palace at Potsdam.

Lack of funds delayed the start of construction, which finally began in 1913. The design comprised two-level, parallel roads six miles (9.6km) in length linked by fast long-radius curves at each end with shallow 1:10 bankings. The roads were 26 ft(8m) wide, separated by an 8 metre grass strip. An unpaid labour force of Russian prisoners of war continued the work during World War 1.

The track was completed in 1921 after financier Hugo Stinnes raised two million marks. It was called *Automobil Verkehrs und Übungstrasse* or Automobile Practice and Traffic Road, thus AVUS or Avus. The first race meeting, a two-day event held in September 1921, was besieged by entries for this exciting new venue on the fringe of Germany's capital.

Germany was about to become engulfed in the massive inflation which virtually destroyed its economy. Racing at the Avus continued in 1922 and 1923 in a minor key with races mainly for sports cars. Makes such as NAG and Fafnir were notable. In 1922 a Fafnir was driven by a young man making his debut, Rudi Caracciola, who a decade later would be one of the leading Grand Prix aces.

After World War 1 Germany was excluded from international motor sport, but in 1925 the AvD was admitted to the Alliance Internationale des Automobile Clubs Reconnus (AIACR), the governing body of motor sport, opening the way for the staging of the first German Grand Prix. Avus was the chosen venue in July 1926.

Realising that the existing 1,500cc GP formula was attracting minimal fields, the AvD promoted a 'touring car' race. This let in thinly disguised racing cars with bolted-on extensions carrying compulsory rear seats. Among the 46 cars entered two 1924 2.0-litre GP Mercedes were driven by Caracciola and Adolf Rosenberger.

During practice a riding mechanic was killed when two cars collided. In the race, Rosenberger led from the start. Then when it rained heavily the asphalt-paved track became slippery and on lap seven Rosenberger slid off the road on the North Curve and hit the timekeepers' box, killing the three occupants.

Left: *Rudi Caracciola and mechanic Eugen Salzer parade their 2.0-litre Mercedes with the winner's garlands after their victory in the 1926 German Grand Prix.*

Manfred von Brauchitsch's SSK Mercedes wins the 1932 Avusrennen, the race commentator starting a legend by calling the streamlined car a 'silvery arrow'.

Numerous crashes badly injured drivers and mechanics, one car skidding across the centre strip and narrowly avoiding a head-on collision with Caracciola's Mercedes. Caracciola stayed on the road and went on to win. An outcry following the chaotic Grand Prix resulted in the suspension of racing at the Avus until 1931.

Racing returned to the Avus in August 1931 with the *Avusrennen* meeting, run on a track where the offending asphalt had been removed to leave bare concrete. Caracciola ran away with the main race in a stripped sports SSKL Mercedes-Benz in front of 200,000 cheering Berliners. He had won the German GP at the Nürburgring with the same car two weeks earlier. Speeds were rising, Caracciola averaging 115mph (185km/h) for the 15-lap race, outpacing the opposition from Bugattis and other Mercedes. Sheer speed made the Avus demanding. In the 10-lap supporting 1,500cc race only two of the 12 starters finished. A local report said that 'one after another was reported as retiring with molten bearings, magneto and other defects'.

It was Mercedes again in 1932. Manfred von Brauchitsch, a nephew of the Field Marshal who was commander-in-chief of the German army in World War 2, fitted his SSKL with an aerodynamic body. This gave him the edge over a much stronger field with works entries from Bugatti and Maserati. The race was marred by a fatal crash when the Czech driver Lobkowicz overturned his Bugatti on the South Curve. In the 1,500cc race the British aristocrat Earl Howe domi-nated in a 1927 GP Delage, winning by the immense margin of three laps.

The Nazis came to power in 1933. The *Avusrennen* featured all the panoply of the New Order with Swastika banners and storm-trooper parades. Hitler attended the 1933 meeting and must have been disappointed. Two aerodynamic SSKL Mercedes were entered. One killed Otto Merz in a practice crash while the other, driven by von Brauchitsch, could not match the speed of the T54 Bugattis, which scored a 1-2. The second-placed T54 was driven by the Polish-French Count Stanislaw Czaikowski. In the supporting voiturette race the German driver 'Bobby' Kohlrausch retired for an odd reason: he was assailed by an attack of cramp.

Two weeks before the *Avusrennen*, Czaikowski had been at the Avus, taking the coveted World Hour Record in his Bugatti. He recorded 132.87mph (213.65km/h) despite having to slow to 80mph (130km/h) for the North and South Curves. Sadly, he was killed later in the 1933 season in a crash at Monza.

For Hitler motor racing was a mechanical manifestation of national virility. As a racing enthusiast he gave every encouragement, directing financial support to Mercedes-Benz and the newly instituted Auto Union to design cars for the 750kg Grand Prix formula which began in

A handsome trophy as presented to the Avus winners in 1932.

Hans Stuck tests
this special Auto
Union record-
breaker in 1935.

At the 1933 meeting the 1,500cc class is about
to start. In the foreground on the left is a
'stromliner' SSKL Mercedes and beside it
two T54 Bugattis. The Bugattis take a 1-2 in
the main race.

Right: In 1934 Rudi Caracciola attacks
international class records with a W25
Mercedes in 1934. The commencement of the
loop leading to the North Curve is seen on the
top right of the image.

1934. Both responded with designs which reduced the opposition to instant obsolescence.

The first public appearance of an Auto Union was in March 1934 when Hans Stuck brought a V16 Type A to the Avus to break Czaikowski's Hour Record, setting a new figure of 134.90mph (217.05km/h). The racing debut of both new models was promised for the *Avusrennen* in May. The Mercedes team was withdrawn with fuel-pump problems but the Auto Unions raced. German hopes were deferred however as the race went to a Tipo B Alfa Romeo with an aerodynamic body driven by Algerian Guy Moll. The sensation of the race was Italian ace Tazio Nuvolari who took fifth place with one leg in plaster, the outcome of a crash a month earlier.

Used only used for one race meeting a year, the Avus was otherwise a part of the rapidly growing Autobahn system. It was closed in October 1934 for Stuck to take some more records. In 1935 the German teams had achieved almost total dominance of Grand Prix racing. The 1935 *Avusrennen* saw full German teams matched against two Bimotore Alfa Romeos from the Scuderia Ferrari, fierce cars with two engines — one in front of the driver and one behind.

Run in two five-lap heats and a ten-lap final, the 1935 race saw speeds previously unattained in racing. The tyres were not up to the pace, needing frequent stops for changes. Stuck won the first heat for Auto Union at 155.60mph (250.36km/h), Caracciola's Mercedes took the second heat. In the final Luigi Fagioli, who had driven his Mercedes to conserve its tyres, came out on top ahead of a Bimotore. His average was 148.20mph (238.45km/h).

The Olympic Games came to Berlin in 1936. When building work on the Olympic stadium cut across the north end of the road a new North Curve was built. This had an imposing 43-degree brick-faced banking. There was no safety wall at the top so it was soon called the 'Wall of Death'.

There were no *Avusrennen* in 1936, though the track was used for part of the Olympic men's marathon and for cycling races. Cars were back in 1937 for the most spectacular race of all. It was a *formule libre* event, so Mercedes and Auto Union pulled out all the stops. Both teams ran several fully aerodynamic cars with larger engines than the normal GP cars.

The meeting had a curtain-raiser 1,500cc race won by a British ERA. The main event was run in two seven-lap heats with an eight-lap final. Caracciola's Mercedes won the first heat from Bernd Rosemeyer's Auto Union by a mere 0.6sec. The second heat went to von Brauchitsch who turned a fastest lap at a staggering 174.83mph (281.3km/h). The pace was telling both on tyres and cars. In the final Hermann Lang came

MANFRED VON BRAUCHITSCH

MANFRED VON BRAUCHITSCH has a place in motor racing history as the first driver of a 'Silver Arrow', the sobriquet by which the German Grand Prix cars of the 1930s are now universally known. Von Brauchitsch was born in 1905, a member of an aristocratic military family. His uncle, *Generalfeldmarschall* Walther von Brauchitsch, was Commander-in-Chief of the German Army from the start of World War 2 until he was sacked by Hitler in December 1941.

An army career for the young Manfred was cut short by serious injuries in a motorcycle accident. He began competing in 1929, driving in hill climbs with a 7.1-litre SSK Mercedes. He first made his mark taking third place at the 1931 Eifelrennen meeting on the legendary Nürburgring.

Having commissioned a streamlined single-seat body for his SSK, von Brauchitsch drove it in the Avus races in 1932. Aided by its smooth cigar shape, gaining extra speed on the ultra-fast track, his silver car beat the recognised aces including Rudi Caracciola driving an Alfa Romeo. Journalist Paul Laven, giving a radio commentary on the race, extolled the victory of the 'silvery arrow'. Thus the legendary name began.

When Mercedes-Benz returned to the Grand Prix world in 1934, von Brauchitsch was a member of the team, wearing a distinctive red skullcap. He went into the history books as the revived team's first victor with a win in the 1934 *Eifelrennen*. After that he suffered a string of misfortunes with both crashes and races lost by mechanical mishaps, some caused by his hard, impetuous driving. He became known as the team's *Pechvögel* or 'unlucky bird'. He didn't score again until the Monaco GP in 1937 and then another win in the French GP in 1938.

Von Brauchitsch spent World War 2 working in a military office in Berlin. After the war, he tried to resume racing without success. While living in West Germany he formed links with the government in East Germany. Charged with espionage, von Brauchitsch fled to East Germany, where he worked for the Ministry of Sport. After the reunification of Germany his pre-war exploits received recognition by Mercedes-Benz. He died in 2003, the last of the great German titans of the 1930s.

through as others dropped back and won in a streamlined Mercedes at the stupendous average of 162.62mph (261.65km/h). Many decades would pass before such a race average would be seen again.

Racing had been dramatic and speeds almost unbelievable, but the Avus was disliked by the drivers. After the thunder and fury of 1937, the 1938 *Avusrennen* were mild affairs. A 2.0-litre sports-car race was a BMW 328 benefit. With motorcycle races, this was run over a shortened circuit of

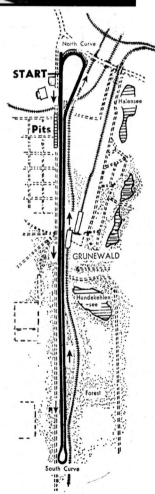

The unique highr-speed Avus circuit in 1954.

Bernd Rosemeyer's Auto Union and Rudi Caracciola's Mercedes share the front row of the grid in the final at the 1935 Avusrennen.

The streamlined Mercedes-Benz of von Brauchitsch and Lang storm past the 'normal' Auto Union of Hasse at the South Curve on the opening lap of the first heat in 1937.

Hermann Lang roars through the North Curve with his special-bodied W125 Mercedes-Benz during the 1937 meeting. He wins at an average of 162mph (259km/h).

5 miles (8km) using the North Banking and a return loop halfway down the main straights.

The South Curve was broken up in 1939 during Autobahn developments, then World War 2 erupted. In the final assault on Berlin in April 1945, one Russian Army advance came through the Grunewald, up the Avus into the city. With the war over, Berlin was divided into four sectors. The Avus lay in the American sector.

Racing returned to the Avus in 1951 over the short 5 mile (8km) course. The *Avusrennen* catered for motorcycles, 500cc racing cars and 2.0-litre Formula 2 cars. To the surprise of drivers from Western Europe, their Ferraris, Gordinis and HWMs were outpaced by BMW-based cars built in the Russian Zone.

In 1952 the Avus held the last round in the West German F2 championship and this time a Ferrari won. It was another Ferrari win in 1953. The supporting race for 500cc cars went to constructor John Cooper driving one of his own cars with bodywork reminiscent of the 1937 Auto Unions. Despite losing time in a first-lap collision, he beat the field at an average of 93.85mph (151.00km/h).

Mercedes-Benz returned to Grand Prix racing in 1954. The W196 was near-invincible, taking Juan Manuel Fangio to his second World Championship. At the end of the season the non-Championship Berlin Grand Prix was run at the Avus. It was as much a political gesture as a sporting event. With Berlin a tendentious issue between Russia and the West, the race was intended to show the hard-pressed West Berliners that they were not forgotten. The race became a Mercedes demonstration, the cars finishing 1-2-3 with 0.9sec covering the trio. Fangio graciously let Karl Kling take the flag.

The repercussions of the Le Mans disaster in 1955 brought German motor racing to a standstill for nearly a year, so racing wasn't resumed at the Avus until 1956, after which two years of sports-car racing followed. A combined sports-car and Formula 2 race in 1958 drew a sizeable field. The winner was the French ace Jean Behra in a Porsche.

Grand Prix racing returned in 1959 when the AvD, perhaps under political pressure and hoping the race-starved Berliners would flock to the course, moved the German Grand Prix from its regular home at the Nürburgring. It was an unpopular move

The Ferraris of Brooks and Gurney and the Coopers of Moss and Brabham share the front row for the first heat of the 1959 German Grand Prix.

Phil Hill's Ferrari Dino 246 chases Graham Hill's Lotus 16 on the North Curve during the 1959 German Grand Prix.

The Grand Prix was run in two 30-lap heats with an aggregated result. The Ferrari Dino 246s were the fastest cars in the race. After the Coopers of Stirling Moss and Jack Brabham dropped out in the first heat, the three Ferraris put on a virtual demonstration, taking 1-2-3 in each heat. The winner was Britain's Tony Brooks who was in hot contention for the World Championship. His average in the first heat was 146.71mph (236.05km/h).

That was the last major race at the Avus. Some minor events were held in subsequent years. In 1968 the North Banking was demolished to make way for local road improvements. The twin straights were used for touring-car races with a rebuilt flat North Curve. After the reunion of East and West Germany, the roads became a major route from Berlin so closure for racing brought increasing problems. The last race was held on the track in 1998. As a race track the Avus became an anachronism but the high speeds achieved on it became a motor-racing legend.

for both entrants and drivers. The North Banking put strains on suspensions that were not encountered on other circuits. The meeting was marred when Jean Behra's sports Porsche went over the top of the banking in a preliminary sports-car race, killing the popular Frenchman.

Porsche sports cars race through the North Curve in 1959, with white lines delineating the 'safe' area.

CHAPTER 5

Barcelona

A publicity poster heralds the 1921 Peñya Rhin Grand Prix at Villafranca.

The triangular circuit of Villafranca, 1921-1922.

Almunia

Monjos

P EÑYA RHIN was an exclusive sporting club which met in a mansion on the Plaza de Cataluña in Barcelona. In 1921 it decided to expand its activities into motor racing. With modesty becoming a beginner, it staged a voiturette race for 1,500cc cars. It nominated a 9.2-mile (14.8km) circuit west of Barcelona. Approximately triangular, made up of rough, tough roads, it ran from the outskirts of the small town of Villafranca. The entry was thin. The most significant was from Bugatti, which sent two of its very successful T13 Brescias. These ran away with the 30-lap race. That winner Pierre de Viscaya took over five hours to complete the course emphasised that it was hard going.

When the race was staged again in 1922 it pulled in a superior field with works teams from Talbot-Darracq, the champions of the voiturette field, Aston Martin and the Italian Chiribiri. The legendary Count Louis Zborowski of 'Chitty Chitty Bang Bang' fame led in an Aston Martin, but had to settle for second place after a puncture. The victor was Kenelm Lee Guinness, the brewery heir, in a Talbot-Darracq.

In 1923 the Peñya Rhin race was held as part of a two-race series with an event at the new banked track at nearby Sitges. Once again it was Talbot-Darracq versus Aston Martin and this time Albert Divo's Talbot Darracq beat Zborowski. Back in fifth place with a Chiribiri was an unknown Italian, Tazio Nuvolari, in one of his first car races. He was to become one of the all-time racing greats.

After its 1923 event the Peñya Rhin did not promote a serious motor race for 10 years. It came back in 1933 with a new 2.35-mile (3.8km) circuit in Montjuïc Park in the centre of Barcelona, overlooking the harbour. For two

Competing on the Villafranca circuit was not for the faint-hearted. Resta's Talbot leads de Vizcaya's Elizade and Zborowski's Aston Martin in the 1923 race.

years it drew a good field of Alfa Romeos and Bugattis and Maseratis. By 1935 the face of Grand Prix racing had changed, becoming the fiefdom of the German Mercedes and Auto Union teams. The Barcelona race was a Mercedes 1-2, pursued all the way by Nuvolari in an outclassed and outpaced Alfa Romeo.

In 1936 Spain was riven by huge political tensions with a left-wing populist government opposed by the right-wing parties and the army. Again this background the race was nevertheless held. Montjuïc Park saw a truly memorable three-cornered contest among Auto Union, Mercedes-Benz and Alfa Romeo. The brilliance of Nuvolari carried the day. He held onto the lead in an ailing and apparently outclassed Alfa Romeo to take the flag ahead of Caracciola's Mercedes.

Four weeks later Spain was plunged into civil war. When it ended in January 1939 the nation was shattered physically and morally. There was little thought of motor racing. Any hope

40

American ace Peter de Paolo is badly hurt when he crashes his Maserati during practice for the 1934 Peñya Rhin Grand Prix.

Above: The new Peñya Rhin circuit of Montjuïc, opened in 1933. It saw racing from 1933 to 1936 and 1966 to 1975.

Rudi Caracciola's W25 Mercedes-Benz passes the museum in the centre of the Montjuïc circuit during the 1935 race.

The season, the first of the newly-instituted World Championship, had found the Alfa Romeo team dominant again. Enzo Ferrari had seen where the future lay, eschewing the supercharger. During 1950 he developed a 4½-litre unblown car which by the end of the season was challenging the Alfa Romeos.

The Alfas stayed away from the non-Championship Barcelona race, but the new Ferraris were there. Also in the field were two of the complex V16 BRMs. After a disastrous debut at Silverstone in August of 1950 the derided BRM team needed a successful European race appearance to silence its critics. In the race the Ferraris won as they pleased with Alberto Ascari leading a 1-2-3. Although showing some pace at the outset, especially in the hands of the doughty Reg Parnell, the BRMs failed dismally.

Luigi Fagioli's W25 Mercedes-Benz is pictured during the 1935 race. He wins at the speed of 66.99mph.

Another cirecuit that ran through the streets of Barcelona was Pedralbes. It was established in 1946, and was essentially used through to 1954.

of a revival faded when World War 2 began nine months later.

The Gran Premio do Peñya Rhin was run again in 1946 as a finale to the first sketchy post-war season. A new circuit, the 3.9-mile (6.27-km) Pedralbes, was chosen running through the streets of Barcelona. Its main feature was a long main straight along the Diagonale, the main thoroughfare of the city, with a return leg through back streets. This fast but bumpy circuit drew a field of 12 starters, a mixed bunch of Maseratis and ERAs. Italian ace Luigi Villoresi led until his Maserati failed which left Italian Giorgio Pelassa in another Maserati to take the flag.

Racing cars were back on the Barcelona streets in 1948. Apart from the all-conquering Alfa Romeo team, all the top GP drivers and cars wore there. It was a Maserati battle which this time Villoresi went on to win followed by Briton Reg Parnell. It was said that 350,000 spectators watched the race.

After another year off, racing was back at the Pedralbes in 1950.

In 1951 the race, awarded the status of Spanish Grand Prix, was the final and deciding round of the World Championship. It lay between Fangio and Ascari; whoever finished in front would be Champion. Ferrari made a wrong decision over tyres — one parameter which has not changed with Formula 1 into the 21st century. The bumps and the speed on the long straight played havoc with the Prancing Horses. Tyres shredded and Fangio sailed into the distance and his first World Championship, leaving a frustrated Ascari in fourth place.

Grand Prix racing at Barcelona dropped out of the calendar for three years. In 1954 the new 2½-litre formula gave a great fillip to the sport with many manufacturers participating. The Spanish Grand Prix returned, the race at Pedralbes the last round of the World Championship. The title had been decided in Fangio's favour beforehand, but six works teams still came for the race.

The new, long-awaited Lancia D50 led the opening laps. Then it became a battle between the Ferrari Squalo of Mike Hawthorn, Maseratis and the Mercedes of Fangio. For once Mercedes was off the pace, its cars overheating when their radiator grilles filled with paper blowing around the straight. Hawthorn carried on unchallenged, scoring the second of his Championship wins. That was the last Pedralbes race. The circuit became a victim of the negative reaction that followed the Le Mans disaster in 1955.

In 1954 Spain's motor club, the RAC de Cataluña, revived

Carretera de Cornella a Fogas De Tordera

Avenida de la Victoria

Paseo de Manuel Girona

Calle de Numancia

START

Pits

Avenida del Generalisimo Franco

Peter Walker's V16 BRM is no match for the Ferraris in the 1950 race. After 33 of the 50 laps he retires with loss of oil from a transaxle design fault.

Several spectators are killed when Franco Rol's 4CLT/48 Maserati spins into the crowd during the 1950 Peñya Rhin GP on the Pedralbes circuit.

Alberto Ascari drives on to win the 1950 Penya Rhin GP on the Pedralbes circuit in his Ferrari 375 F1.

Fangio takes his 159 Alfa Romeo to victory in the 1951 Grand Prix. This was the last win for the incredible 158/159 Alfa after eight seasons of racing.

The battle of the titans: Fangio's Alfa 158 leads the 375 F1 Ferrari of Ascari and the Alfa of Bonetto into the corner at the end of the Avenida del General Franco during the opening laps of the 1951 Spanish Grand Prix. Crowd protection is non-existent.

Fangio's 159 Alfa is flat out on the Avenida del General Franco during the 1951 Grand Prix. This was one of the more impressive settings for a circuit. It is now called Avinguda Diagonale.

Fangio takes the flag in the 1951 Spanish Grand Prix. This was the last race of the 1500cc supercharged and 4500cc unsupercharged Formula 1.

the Montjuïc Park circuit with a low-key minor meeting offering a series of GT races. To local delight the main race was won by an exotic Barcelona-built Pegaso. The local GT races continued annually, with some gaps, until 1966. Then after a hiatus of 30 years the single-seaters returned to Montjuïc Park.

The original circuit was used for the Formula 2 Gran Premio de Barcelona. Attracting all the leading drivers, including past and current World Champions Jim Clark, Jack Brabham and Jackie Stewart, Formula 2 reigned in Montjuïc Park for three years. The enthusiasm of the Cataluña club then paid off when, in 1969, the circuit saw the Spanish Grand Prix return to Barcelona as a round of the World Championship.

At that time Formula 1 was racing down a technical cul-de-sac with all the cars carrying absurd front and rear wings. During the race the rear wing on the Lotus of World Champion Graham Hill collapsed and he crashed heavily, though he was unhurt. His team-mate Jochen Rindt was leading the race until his wing also collapsed at the same point on the circuit and his car hit Hill's wrecked Lotus. Amid the chaos Stewart carried on to win by two laps in his Matra. The outcome of the accidents was the FIA's immediate ban on wings.

Barcelona was alternating with the Jarama circuit at Madrid in staging the Spanish Grand Prix, so Formula 2 cars filled the off-years. For the Spanish Grand Prix in 1973 Montjuïc

JACK BRABHAM

AFTER winning the midget-car championship in his home country, Australian Jack Brabham came to England in 1955 to seek his motor-racing fortune. His was a fairy-tale story fuelled by sheer hard graft and shrewd ingenuity.

Brabham worked for racing-car manufacturer Cooper as a mechanic, began racing Coopers and went on to take the World Championship in 1959 and 1960. A remarkably inventive and intuitive development engineer, Brabham became frustrated by the conservative approach of John and Charles Cooper. In 1962 he broke away to build his own cars with the help of engineer Ron Tauranac.

Brabham began with the emerging Formula 3. Soon he moved back to his natural metier, Formula 1. In 1966 he won the Championship again, becoming the first and only driver to become World Champion in a car bearing his name.

Like most of his top-rank contemporaries, Brabham also drove in Formula 2. This supporting formula gave a chance for up-and-coming drivers to match their skills against the leading Grand Prix drivers. A full Formula 2

calendar ran throughout the racing season. Unlike most of his rivals, who used the British Cosworth engine, Brabham had done a deal with Honda, who started slowly but soon caught up.

When the AC Cataluña reopened the Montjuic circuit in 1966, all the leading Formula 2 contenders appeared. The field included three World Champions and two future Champions. It was wet. The rain in Spain may have been mainly on the plain, but it fell heavily in Barcelona that day. On the results earlier in the season, it looked a likely win for Jackie Stewart in a Matra. The Scot took an early lead, tailed by the canny Brabham in one of his own cars.

Conditions behind Brabham were causing problems for many drivers. With two-thirds of the forty-lap race run, Stewart came into the pits with a flat battery. It was changed but its replacement was also sparkless. By the time a second battery had been found and fitted, Brabham was in front. He romped home with a lead of nearly a minute to take the first major race on the Montjuïc circuit for 30 years.

By the end of the season Brabham had pulled off a double triumph. As well as becoming World Champion in Formula 1, he also secured the European Formula 2 title.

Park had been resurfaced, making it faster. In the 1970s the modern pattern was emerging where top Formula 1 drivers stuck to that category alone. The Formula 2 Montjuïc field no longer pulled the top aces.

When the Spanish Grand Prix returned to Montjuïc Park in 1975 the drivers refused to practise on the circuit as the Armco barriers were loose, inadequately bolted. Eventually the work was done — drivers and crews pitching in — but some drivers were still unhappy. World Champion Emerson Fittipaldi refused to race. In the race two drivers pulled off after a lap saying it was unsafe. Rolf Stommelen was leading after 25 laps when a rear wing collapsed. His car hit another competitor and flew over the barriers, killing four spectators and a marshal. The race was stopped a few laps later and McLaren-mounted Jochen Mass declared the winner.

It was the end of serious motor racing at Montjuïc Park. An indication of how speeds in Grand Prix racing had risen over 40 years was that in 1933 Nuvolari turned the Park's fastest lap in 133 seconds while in 1973 the ultimate lap record was set by Ronnie Peterson in only 83 seconds.

The Spanish Grand Prix continued to be held on other circuits. In 1989 work began on a new purpose-built track at Montmeló, about 15 miles (20km) north-east of Barcelona, called the Circuit de Cataluña. With a lap distance of 2.95 miles (4.74km) in 1991 it was ready to become the permanent home of the Spanish Grand Prix. A circuit much in the modern idiom, it offers few opportunities for overtaking but has magnificent facilities and good spectating. It has become the regular circuit for official pre-season Formula 1 testing.

At the Circuit de Cataluña's first race in 1991 a win would have made Ayrton Senna World Champion, but he made a wrong tyre choice. He had a legendary wheel-to-wheel contest with Nigel Mansell on the main straight where the bravest braked last. BBC TV commentator Murray Walker nearly had apoplexy! Senna fell back, leaving the Briton to take the flag.

In 1992 the Spanish Grand Prix was held in May, becoming an early Championship round, and has remained so since. It was Mansell's year bringing the third of a straight run of five wins taking him to the World Championship.

The beginning of the 1994 season was marred by the death of Ayrton Senna at Imola. The RAC de Cataluña, fearing a similar accident, eased one of the fastest bends on the back straight. Damon Hill, son of two-times Champion Graham Hill, had moved up into Senna's place as the no 1 driver in the Williams-Renault team and was facing a new kid on the block, German Michael Schumacher in a Benetton-Ford. Hill won at Cataluña, but it was Schumacher who took his first Championship.

At Cataluña in 1996 Schumacher's drive was one of the best in his remarkable career. His Ferrari was handling badly, but it was a wet day. He coped with the conditions in a way his rivals couldn't match, scoring a resounding win.

Mercedes-Benz had returned to the Grand Prix world in 1995, funding British-made, Mercedes-labelled engines which were supplied to McLaren, starting a relationship which has continued to the present day. After a shaky start the marriage became fruitful with the McLaren-Mercedes taking Finn Mika Häkkinen and Scot David Coulthard to first and second places in the 1998 Spanish Grand Prix. The pair ran a repeat performance in 1999 and then made it a hat-trick in 2000.

The triumphant years of Schumacher and Ferrari commenced. He had a lucky Cataluña win in 2001 but was indomitable in 2002 and 2003, leading for every lap to take both

Following the end of serious motor racing at the Montjuïc circuit in 1975, work started on a new purpose-built track 15 miles north-east of Barcelona in 1989. Called the Circuit de Cataluña, it opened in 1991 and is now the current home of the Spanish Grand Prix.

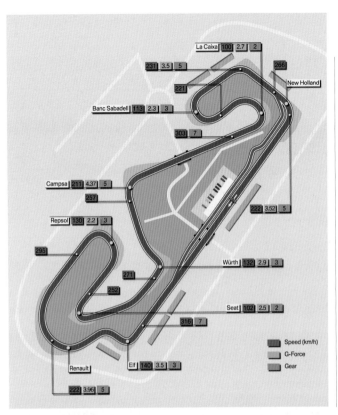

La Caixa 100 2.7 2

231 3.5 5

266

New Holland

221

Banc Sabadell 113 2.3 3

303 7

Campsa 211 4.37 5

257

222 3.52 5

Repsol 130 2.2 3

295

Würth 132 2.9 3

271

252

Seat 102 2.5 2

316 7

Renault

Elf 140 3.5 3

222 3.96 5

Speed (km/h)
G-Force
Gear

wins. He did it again in 2004. That year the line of the Caixa corner behind the pits, was changed, reducing the lap distance to 2.86 miles (4.62km) so the race distance was increased by a lap to 66 laps.

Though some think the circuit boring, that didn't concern the Spanish crowd in 2006. To huge delight, local hero Fernando Alonso was the winner, the first Spanish victor of the national race, en route to his first World Championship. To complete the Spanish joy he took a second Championship in 2007. Racing at Cataluña can be predictable. In 2009 Jenson Button was the ninth successive driver to win from pole position.

The Circuit de Cataluña is now the epicentre of Spanish motor sport. It hosts rounds of the Moto GP championship, 24-hour motorcycle races and many national meetings. In 2008 a 1,000km round of the Le Mans series for sports-racing cars gave a win to a diesel-powered Peugeot 908. Despite its limitations as a stage for dramatic racing, it is ideal for television broadcasting and, above all, safe for the competitors. For Spanish enthusiasts it has become an annual pilgrimage.

The start of the Spanish Grand Prix at Cataluña in 2000 sees Ferraris, McLarens and a Williams jockeying for position.

Schneider's Mercedes-Benz leads the pack in a round of the 2006 DTM Championship at Cataluña.

Rosberg's Williams leads a group of cars during the 2006 Grand Prix at Cataluña. The massed ranks of spectators are impressive.

Nico Rosberg leaves the pits in his Williams-Cosworth FW28 during practice for the 2006 Spanish Grand Prix.

CHAPTER 6

Monza

The field lines up for the start of the 1922 Italian Grand Prix, the first major event at Monza. The junction of the banked track and the road circuit can be seen.

L IKE Le Mans, Monza is one of the most evocative words in European motor sports, and with good reason. For some 90 years it has been by far the most important circuit in a nation that is passionate about motor racing.

The first Italian Grand Prix in 1921 was organised by the Automobile Club of Milan on a long road circuit at Brescia. Using public roads made the collection of admission fees problematical, so the club resolved to build a dedicated track near Milan. A site was found in the Royal Park of Monza about 10 miles (16km) north-east of Milan.

In a context familiar in the 21st century, there were environmental objections. Once these were overcome, an artificial road circuit and a shallow banked speed track were built in 110 days. The speed track was 3 miles (4.5km) long, with shallow bankings with a maximum height of 8½ft (2.6m). The road circuit had a lap of 3.4 miles (5.5km). Both shared a common main straight flanked by grandstands on the outside and pits and paddock on the infield. A combined lap using both parts was 6.2 miles (10km).

The first race held in September 1922 was a 60-lap event for *voiturettes*, using both parts of the track. It was a Fiat 1-2-3-4 with Pietro Bordino the winner. A week later the 80-lap Italian Grand Prix was held over the same course. Fiat dominated the 1922 Grand Prix field so a second win for the talented Bordino was no surprise.

A revolutionary rear-engined Type RH Benz is followed by a Miller on Monza's shallow banking during the 1923 Italian Grand Prix.

Monza was well-used from the beginning. As well as testing, in 1922 and in 1923 there were motorcycle and touring car races. The first British success came in 1923 when Arthur Waite's Austin Seven took the flag in the Cyclecar Grand Prix. The 1923 season finished with the Italian Grand Prix. It was won by Fiat again, using the new-fangled supercharger which gave a huge advantage, especially on a fast circuit.

In 1924 Alfa Romeo nudged Fiat from the top of the tree. The P2 Alfas swept the board in 1924 and 1925, finishing both seasons with sweeping wins in the Italian Grand Prix. The 1924 race saw the death of Count Louis Zborowski in an ill-handling Mercedes. The Monza race was becoming the high-speed dash which ended the Grand Prix season.

The first non-Italian GP win came with a Bugatti victory in 1926. In the Monza motorcycle races Tazio Nuvolari and Achille Varzi were gaining the major honours. Both would soon become equally prominent in the car world. French success continued in 1927 when Robert Benoist swept to victory in his Delage during his triumphal season.

It nearly all ended abruptly in September 1928. In Monza's European Grand Prix Emilio Materassi was one of a group duelling for the lead when his Talbot swerved off the track and into the grandstand enclosure. He was killed, as were 27 spectators. Racing continued at Monza in 1929 after many changes were made to ensure greater safety for the spectators.

The current GP formula was attracting few entries, so in 1929 the Italian Grand Prix was abandoned. A *formule libre* Monza Grand Prix was run on the banked track with several eliminating heats and a final. The Monza Grand Prix was run again in 1930, but used a circuit with the southern banking and half the road section which became known as the Florio circuit. It brought one of the first major wins for rapidly improving Maserati.

Monza was already establishing a reputation as one of the faster tracks. The banked track had been lapped at 124mph (200km/h) in 1929 and the combined course used in 1930 was lapped at 102mph (165km/h).

The Italian Grand Prix returned in 1931. Ten hours' duration and run over the full road and banked track, it was a gruelling fight between the new 8C Alfa Romeos and the Bugattis. Driven by aces Nuvolari and Giuseppe Campari, who doubled race driving with opera singing, an Alfa triumphed and thereafter was called the 'Monza' model. In 1932, when the Grand Prix was reduced to a more practical five hours, Alfa Romeo triumphed again, bringing out its revolutionary monoposto Tipo B which gave racing-car design a handsome new face.

The 1933 season was black. The Italian Grand Prix and the free-formula Monza Grand Prix were run on the same rain-soaked day in September. The Grand Prix was run in the morning, over the full combined course, and the Monza GP in the afternoon on the banked track.

The Grand Prix was a typical Alfa/Maserati/Bugatti battle with the Alfa of Fagioli coming out on top. In the second heat of the Monza GP Borzacchini took the lead on the first lap. On the south banking Campari, who had declared it was his last race before retirement, went ahead but lost control, going over the top of the banking. Borzacchini braked hard to miss the Alfa and his Maserati also went over the top. Both drivers were killed. After a two-hour delay the cars came out for the final. Franco-Polish Count Stanislaw Czaikowski went into the lead in his Bugatti. On lap nine he too lost control, went over the top of the banking and died when his car overturned and caught fire.

The dangers of the banked track having been realised, the full banked lap was not used again. In 1934 Grand Prix racing had changed irrevocably with the arrival of a new set of rules under which the Auto Union and Mercedes dominated. For that

year's Italian Grand Prix an odd and potentially dangerous circuit was created. It used the main straight on which cars ran in both directions, merely separated by a row of cones, round the south banking where there was a permanent chicane and returned via a link road to the Parabolica curve, thence to the main straight. In spite of this obvious attempt to handicap them the Germans won, a Mercedes leading home an Auto Union with the Alfas and Maseratis trailing behind.

The Florio circuit was used for the 1935 Grand Prix with a rash of chicanes intended to give the Italian cars a chance. It didn't work, though Italy might have prevailed had Alfa Romeo not made some injudicious driver-swaps. The Florio circuit with even more pronounced chicanes was used again

The 16-cylinder V4 Maserati driven by builder Alfieri Maserati prepares for the third heat of the 1929 Monza Grand Prix beside the stripped sports SS Mercedes-Benzes of Calflisch, Rosenberg and Momberger.

Nuvolari's Tipo B Alfa Romeo is paraded before the start of the 1932 Monza Grand Prix.

Race-winner Rudi Caracciola takes his W25 Mercedes through one of the chicanes in the 1934 Grand Prix in front of a Tipo B Alfa and Nuvolari's Tipo 34 Maserati.

in 1936. Alfa hopes were high as Mercedes, having a disastrous season, had pulled out, but the Auto Unions were too quick.

Local politics intervened in 1937. No major car races took place at Monza though, as always, there was a full season of motorcycle racing. In 1938 an Italian win was celebrated in the Grand Prix run on the Florio circuit, but it was Nuvolari in an Auto Union. The supporting race for 1,500cc voiturettes brought a resounding win for the new Tipo 158 Alfas, but the race was marred as law student Aldo Marazza was killed when he left the road in his Maserati on the slowing-down lap.

A major reconstruction started in 1939 included the demolition of the banked track. The road circuit was realigned and extended at its southern end. It should have been completed for the Italian Grand Prix in September of 1939 but World War 2 intervened. The work was finished in the summer of 1940. By then Italy was in the war, though the new 3.9-mile (6.3-km) circuit was used in 1941 by Alfa Romeo for development and testing. Towards the end of the war, when it was used for storing military vehicles, much damage was done. Political pressures tried to force the abandonment of Monza. The AC of Milan fought a successful battle and in 1948 the road circuit was restored, following the 1940 layout.

The inaugural meeting, the Autodrome Grand Prix, was held in October 1948 and saw the all-conquering team of Tipo 158 Alfas finish 1-2-3-4. In second place was Count Felice Trossi, mortally ill with cancer which killed him only months later. During a full season in 1949 a Formula 2 race was won by rising star Juan Manuel Fangio. Ferrari took its first Italian Grand Prix at the end of the season.

After a sabbatical year the Alfa team was back in 1950, when it swept the board in the first year of the World Championship. Alfa's supremacy ended in 1951, when the team were beaten by Alberto Ascari's Ferrari in the Grand Prix. Monza hummed with activity with many meetings for car and motorcycles, testing and even a special stage for the Alpine Rally.

By the early 1950s the Grand Prix season was culminating with the Italian Grand Prix in September. During the 2.0-litre

Hermann Müller thrust his Auto Union into the front row of the 1938 Italian GP alongside the Mercedes-Benz trio. The latter faded, leaving Nuvolari on Auto Union the winner.

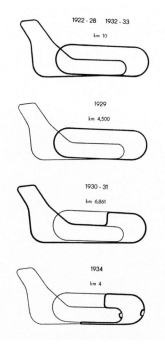

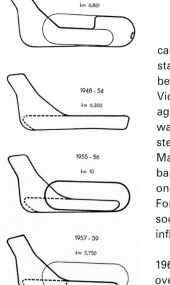

formula 1953 Grand Prix a furious slipstreaming battle between the Ferraris and Maseratis peaked on the last corner of the last lap. Ascari spun, discommoding several other rivals. This let Fangio slip through to win with a Maserati, but Ascari took the Championship.

Mercedes-Benz came back to Monza in 1954 when the 2½-litre GP formula began, manifesting the prowess it had demonstrated 20 years earlier with Fangio taking the Grand Prix after Stirling Moss's leading Maserati retired. In June 1954 Monza hosted its first major long-distance sports-car race, the 1,000km *Supercortemaggiore* GP which was an inevitable Ferrari win.

At the end of 1954 bulldozers and contractors moved in again. A new banked track was built with a lap of 2.63 miles (4.25km). The northern banking was on the site of the 1922 original but the southern was moved inwards. The banking was 20ft (6.2m) high and designed to suit a lap speed of 160mph (258km/h). Its top was protected by strong guard rails. The road was redesigned be used in conjunction with the banked track. The Parabolica curve was altered, but the overall lap distance remained at 6.2 miles (10km). The new circuit was ready for the 1955 season

All Italy mourned when Alberto Ascari was killed testing a sports Ferrari at Monza in May 1955, only days after his Lancia had crashed into the harbour at Monaco. Mercedes came back again in 1955, racing on the full road circuit and banked track, and took the Grand Prix once more, giving Fangio his third Championship. The banked track had became a popular venue for record-breaking.

In an imaginative promotion, American drivers with their Indy roadsters were invited in June 1957 for the Monza '500'. This was a flat-out blind on the banked track in three 63-lap heats and billed as Europe versus the USA. The race drew few European entries apart from three Ecurie Ecosse D-type Jaguars. It was an American victory with the fastest lap set at 175.7mph (282.8km/h). It was an indication that the balance of power in Formula 1 was shifting when the 1957 Grand Prix over the road circuit was won by Moss's British Vanwall.

Ferrari and Maserati came to the 1958 '500', which staged a spectacular battle between the two continents. Victory went to the USA again. In the third heat Moss was lucky to escape when the steering broke on his Maserati at full speed on the banking. The same year saw one of the first races for Formula Junior, which was soon to become a big influence in racing.

Politics loomed again in 1960. The Grand Prix was run over the combined road and track circuit. The British teams complained that the pounding of the banked track could cause suspension failures. Their successful boycott of the race caused much ill-feeling. When in 1961 the race was again held on the combined circuit, the British teams overcame their reluctance and appeared. During the second lap Jim Clark's Lotus collided with Wolfgang von Trips's Ferrari under braking for the Parabolica turn. The Ferrari crashed into the crowd, killing von Trips and 15 spectators. It was the last Grand Prix on the banked track. After that, only the road circuit was used.

The era of the great slipstreaming Italian Grands Prix had begun with groups of cars battling for the lead only lengths apart. It was an epoch that brought wins for British drivers and cars. In 1965 serious sports-car racing returned with a 1,000-km race over the full combined circuit, a round in the Manufacturers' Championship. Italian honour was satisfied by a Ferrari win. Like Brooklands and Montlhéry before it, the

*Left: **Monza circuit development from 1922 to 1959.***

Contemporary circuit map of Monza in 1957.

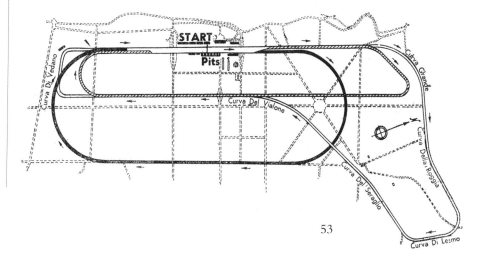

Ferraris and Maseratis fight wheel-to-wheel all the way in the 1953 Grand Prix. Fangio (Maserati), the eventual winner, leads the Ferraris of Farina and Ascari through the Parabolica curve.

The Alfa Romeo mechanics practise a pit stop before the 1950 Italian Grand Prix.

The full-bodied W196 Mercedes of Stirling Moss leads the similar car of Juan Manuel Fangio on the banked track in the early laps of the 1955 Grand Prix.

Monza banked track had deteriorated and the 1969 1,000-km event witnessed its end for racing.

In a world where commercial sponsorship was starting to infiltrate Formula 1, the 1970 Grand Prix was overshadowed by the death of Jochen Rindt in a practice accident. He became the first posthumous World Champion. A year later Peter Gethin's BRM took the flag by the narrowest margin of 0.01sec after a race-long slipstream fight.

Fears of an inevitable accident led to the end of the slipstreaming races in 1972 with the introduction of chicanes. In 1971 a Porsche 917 had lapped the road circuit at 153.12mph (246.42km/h). This was nearly as quick as the fastest lap in the 1971 Grand Prix at 153.39mph (247.01km/h) so something had to give, though chicanes did not appear for the 1,000-km race until 1974.

More chicanes appeared in 1976, establishing the present pattern of the circuit. Despite the changes another tragedy in 1978 saw Swede Ronnie Peterson die after his Lotus was in a collision at the chicane after the pits. In 1980 politics and criticism of ageing facilities at Monza saw the Grand Prix move from Monza to Imola. Renovations and improvements bought it back in 1981.

Over the years Monza has run the 1,000-km, under different guises, as rounds in the Manufacturers', Endurance and Sports Prototype championships. Jaguar, Porsche, McLaren and Peugeot saw the winner's circle. In 1980 came a win for the record book when the successful Lola-Ford was co-driven by South African woman driver Desiré Wilson.

'God Save the Queen' rang out across Monza in 1991, celebrating Nigel Mansell's win, and it was heard again to honour Damon Hill in 1993 and 1994. The Monza *tifosi*, the fans whose banners and flags impart the atmosphere of a medieval joust, are fiercely patriotic. National feelings were put aside when Michael Schumacher joined Ferrari in 1996, becoming their acclaimed hero. When a red car wins the crowds invade the track; Schumacher gave them every opportunity.

*Left: **Monza circuit development from 1957 to 1975.***

The Ferrari of Wolfgang von Trips and the Lotus of Jim Clark collided on the second lap of the 1961 Grand Prix. Von Trips and fourteen spectators were killed.

One of the Ecurie Ecosse D-type Jaguars is pushed to the start ahead of a 4.5-litre Ferrari before the 1958 'Race of Two Worlds'.

RONNIE PETERSON

SWEDE Ronnie Peterson was one of the generation of drivers who graduated from Formula 3. Unlike most of his rivals Peterson did not drive a British Formula 3 car. Instead he chose an Italian Tecno painted yellow and sponsored by cough-sweet maker 'Smog'. He showed an uncanny mastery of his car under all conditions.

The Swede's talent was soon spotted. Peterson raced for the relatively unsuccessful March Formula 1 team until 1973, then moved into the big time when Colin Chapman recruited him for Team Lotus. His team-mate Emerson Fittipaldi seemed set to become Champion, but Peterson scored three wins. When the teams arrived at Monza, Fittipaldi had to win the Italian GP to keep his hopes alive. Peterson upset Fittipaldi's applecart by taking the win, beating him to the line in a slipstream battle by a mere 0.8sec.

In 1974 Fittipaldi moved to McLaren. Peterson stayed with Lotus where he raced the now ageing Type 72. At Monza Fittipaldi must have had a true sense of deja vu. He received the same treatment from Peterson, remarkably with a gap that was again 0.8 second. Lotus was having an off spell so Peterson abandoned Chapman's team at the end of 1975 and went back to the struggling March.

Ronnie Peterson had a dismal 1976, racing a car which was well off the pace. It came good at Monza, though. In mid-race the rains came. The drivers were signalled that the race was about to be halted so the cars could change to rain tyres. The signal to stop did not appear...and did not appear. While his rivals slowed, waiting for the signal, Peterson pressed on. He was too far ahead to be caught by the time the rest realised that the race wasn't being stopped.

After a season with Tyrrell, Peterson went back to Lotus for 1978. With two wins and a string of second places he arrived at Monza with a real chance of becoming World Champion. For safety a chicane had been built at Monza between the start and Curva Grande, the first corner. After a bungle by the starter the cars at the rear of the grid were rolling when the green light was shown. Collisions resulted when the bunched-up field entered the chicane. Ronnie Peterson's Lotus was rammed.

Though his leg was broken, Peterson's injuries were not thought to be serious. Complications set in, however, and he died a few hours later. Immensely popular, Peterson surely had the talent to become a World Champion. Sweden had lost a hero.

In their BMW Saubers, Robert Kubica and Nick Heidfeld lead the scramble around the first chicane in the 2007 Italian Grand Prix.

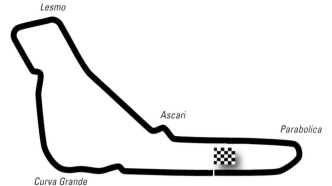

Monza circuit from 1976 to 2009.

In 2002 Schumacher had already clinched the Championship when the teams came to Monza. There had been outrage when his team-mate Rubens Barrichello slowed to let him pass and take the flag in Austria. At Monza Schumacher seemed to hang back to return the compliment to Barrichello. There were no doubts next year, when Schumacher led from flag to flag.

Though the golden years for Ferrari were ending, in 2006 Schumacher took the flag again, his 90th win in Championship races. He then announced that he was retiring at the end of the season. History was made in 2008 when German Sebastian Vettel led all the way to score his first F1 win and the first for the previously struggling Toro Rosso team.

At 21 years Vettel was the youngest driver to win a Championship race. Barrichello may have been given the 2002 race, but there were no doubts about his resounding win in 2009 with a Brawn-Mercedes.

From its inception Monza has seen more drama, triumphs and tragedies than almost any other circuit. Its unique atmosphere is charged with the emotion of the massed partisan Italian fans. They throng to Monza every year, always hoping and cheering for a red car to take the flag.

The winning Peugeot 908 leads the field through the chicane after the start in the 2008 Le Mans Series Championship race.

Lewis Hamilton pilots his McLaren-Mercedes MP4/24 during the 2009 Italian Grand Prix. He spins on the last lap and is unplaced.

CHAPTER 7

Spa-Francorchamps

Winner of the 1927 24-Hours, the Excelsior-Albert I driven by Sénéchal and Caerels makes a pit stop. The track has a primitive rough surface in its early days.

Far right: **Louis Chiron's Tipo B Alfa leads the T59 Bugatti of René Dreyfus into Eau Rouge at the start of the 1934 Grand Prix. Dreyfus is the winner, scoring the last major Grand Prix victory for Bugatti.**

U NTIL the early years of the 20th century the sleepy town of Spa, in Belgium's Liège province, was virtually unknown save for the beneficial qualities of its natural spring waters. It burst onto the world scene during World War 1 when it was the headquarters of Kaiser Wilhelm II. Despite the war, Spa's Ardennes district suffered little.

In 1920 three motoring enthusiasts, Jules de Their, Henri Langlois van Orphem and Raymond de Tornaco, were looking for a suitable site for a major national circuit. They found a rough triangle of roads linking the towns of Spa-Francorchamps, Malmédy and Stavelot. Though rough and narrow, the roads offered a sporting course of 9.3 miles (14.9km). Parts of the circuit ran through open country, but much of it swooped and climbed through the Ardennes forests.

A motorcycle Grand Prix was held on the circuit in 1921. A car race was arranged but a muddle over dates and publicity produced no entries, so no race. Better planning by the RACB (Royal Automobile Club de Belgique) produced a 40-lap touring-car race in 1922, won by an Imperia driven by de Tornaco. In 1924 the RACB, doubtless inspired by the success of the Le Mans 24-hour race, put on a day-long race of its own. It drew an entry of 27, comparable with Le Mans. Victory went to a Bignan.

In 1925 the RACB, noting the success of the French, Spanish and Italian races, moved up a gear and promoted the first Belgian Grand Prix. Placed early in the season, only the Alfa Romeo and Delage teams were ready. Ettore Bugatti cheekily said he couldn't afford to send a team to Belgium! It was a total Alfa walk-over, the team's cars of Ascari and Campari the only ones still running over the race's last 25 laps.

To spite a crowd that had been unkind to his red cars, their designer Vittorio Jano arranged to have his lunch served on a table plunked in front of the pits.

After 1926, when its formula changed to 1½-litre cars, Grand Prix racing received little support from manufacturers and indeed from organisers such as the RACB which had little justification for putting on races. The Spa 24 Hours flourished though. It was run a few weeks after Le Mans, which gave a chance of redemption for failures in the French race. Alfa Romeo was establishing credentials with its sports-racing cars and several Spa 24-hour wins were notched up.

GP cars came back to Spa in 1930 for the Grand Prix of Europe, run to a bizarre fuel-consumption formula. It became a virtual demonstration for the Bugatti team, but the crowd booed the result. The team number two, Bouriat, led to the line on the last lap, then stopped to let his number one, Louis Chiron, go past to take the flag.

In 1931 the 10-hour Grand Prix was the last round of the European Championship. It began at 7:00 am and ended with a Bugatti win by virtue of much slicker pitwork. The German teams should have been at Spa in 1934 but a customs row over imported special fuel blocked their arrival. Their absence saw a small and poignant piece of history. The race was won by René Dreyfus's Bugatti, the last Bugatti win in a major Grand Prix.

The 24-Hour series continued to 1938, with some gap years, but usually providing an Alfa Romeo benefit. Spa's races had a much wider spread of entries than Le Mans. Some quite mundane cars raced at Spa, sometimes surprising with unexpected speed and endurance. The German teams must have paid the custom duties as they raced in the 1935 and 1937 Grands Prix. They swept the board in both years with Mercedes and Auto Union dividing the wins.

During the two decades after Spa was opened the circuit's roads were improved and widened. The start line and pits were situated just after the La Source hairpin, the nearest point to Spa. The cars charged downhill, across a small bridge and then turned left to a hairpin. This was the Old Customs House corner, the site of such a post when the Belgian-German border ran nearby.

In the 1935 Grand Prix, the W25 Mercedes of von Brauchitsch leads the T59 Bugatti of Benoist on the uphill climb to Burnenville.

Top left: In the 1930s Spa's 24 Hours draws a wide selection of cars. At the start of the 1934 race a Hudson leads away while in the line-up are a Bentley, Buick, Hotchkiss and Studebaker.

Richard Seaman takes the Stavelot Hairpin in heavy rain in his Mercedes at the 1939 Belgian Grand Prix.

In 1939 a new section, the Eau Rouge-Raidillon, was built to cut out the old hairpin. Reducing the lap to 9.0 miles (14.5km), it created a fast uphill curve after the pits. Still used today, it is regarded by many top drivers as the most challenging bend on any circuit. The Raidillon was used for the first time in the 1939 Grand Prix. It was a tragic race. The British ace Richard Seaman crashed his Mercedes while leading in heavy rain. It caught fire and he died from burns soon after.

The circuit was unaffected by World War 2 until December 1944. It was in the core of the last German offensive in the

Richard (Dick) Seaman's Mercedes burns after it spun off in the rain in the 1939 GP. Seaman died from his burns soon after.

West, through the Ardennes, which became known as the 'Battle of the Bulge'.

A German SS division pushed north from Stavelot toward a US fuel depot sited near the present pits. The fuel was essential for the German army if its advance were to continue. The attack was repulsed with heavy losses on both sides. America's General Patton made his temporary HQ at Malmedy.

Racing returned to Spa in 1947. The Belgian Grand Prix was dominated by the Alfa Romeo team which was carrying all before it. Revived in 1948, the 24 Hours saw an unexpected Aston Martin win, the first international British success in the

The Tipo 158 Alfas dominate the 1947 Grand Prix. Achille Varzi lines up for La Source followed by Jean-Pierre Wimille at the site of the current pits complex. The bend in the background is the scene of Dick Seaman's fatal crash in 1939.

The Tipo 159 Alfas of Fangio and Farina are gridded ahead of the Tipo 375 F1 Ferraris of Ascari and Taruffi before the 1951 Grand Prix.

post-war years. French pride was satisfied in the 1949 Grand Prix when middle-aged Louis Rosier in his Lago-Talbot beat the Ferraris, but a Ferrari won the 24 Hours.

The fastest section of the circuit was the two-mile Masta straight which was not in fact straight as it had a kink in the middle which only the bravest took flat out. During the 1950 Grand Prix, Luigi Fagioli was timed in his Alfa Romeo on the Masta at 200.75mph (323.27km/h). Spa was vying with Reims in France to claim the glory of the fastest circuit in Europe. In 1950, pursuing this aim, the Stavelot Hairpin was removed and replaced by a long slightly banked curve. This reduced the lap to 8.7 miles (14km) but speeds went up as desired. Over 30 seconds came off the faster lap times.

Fangio showed his mastery in 1954 when the front suspension of his Maserati collapsed. He nursed the stricken car, its nose rubbing on the ground, to the flag and victory. Spa stayed ahead in the speed competition with Reims. In 1958 Mike Hawthorn did the fastest lap in the Grand Prix at

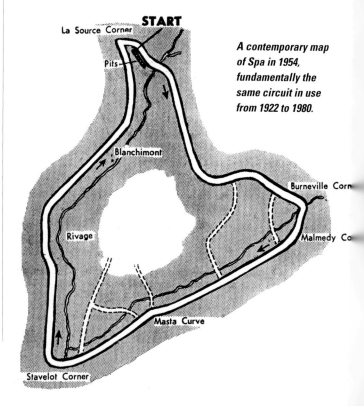

A contemporary map of Spa in 1954, fundamentally the same circuit in use from 1922 to 1980.

Veteran Louis Rosier takes his Lago-Talbot around La Source on the way to an unheralded win in the 1949 Belgian Grand Prix.

Alberto Ascari and his F2 Ferrari 500 dominate the 1952 season. Here he takes the La Source hairpin on his way to victory at Spa.

Stirling Moss (Maserati 250F) leads the field through Eau Rouge at the start of the 1956 Belgian Grand Prix.

132.36mph (213.01km/h). After the 1953 race, a round in the World Sports Car Championship, the 24-Hours disappeared from the calendar for the rest of the 1950s. In its place a series of sports and touring-car races was run annually. These drew big fields of top-line and amateur drivers, many from Britain.

A hero of the British racing scene at that time was Archie Scott-Brown. Despite major physical disabilities he had risen to the top of the ladder, even competing in Formula 1. In 1958 he drove a Lister-Jaguar in the Spa sports-car race. Fighting for the lead, he lost control at the same corner as Dick Seaman. The Lister may have struck the Seaman memorial stone as it overturned and caught fire. Scott-Brown died of burns soon afterwards.

Spa hosted another tragic meeting in 1960. Stirling Moss crashed his Lotus and was badly hurt during the Grand Prix practice when the suspension broke. Worse still, on race day Chris Bristow in a Cooper and Alan Stacey in a Lotus were both killed in crashes. Stacey crashed after being hit in the face by a bird. He was a promising driver; not many knew he had an artificial leg.

The weather has always been an important factor in racing at Spa. Amid the hills and forests, it can be fine on one part of the circuit but raining heavily on another. In 1966 this variability was instrumental in bringing about a major change to Formula 1. The Grand Prix starting grid was dry. When the field reached Malmedy on the opening lap the rain poured down and six cars went off. When the Masta kink was reached two more departed, including Jackie Stewart's BRM. It overturned into a ditch with the driver trapped underneath.

Soaked with fuel, Stewart waited for some time before being released with a broken shoulder. The crash inspired Stewart to start a campaign for greater safety in Formula 1, setting in train many of the reforms that have come since. Stirling Moss said, 'Spa was daunting and frightening

JIM CLARK

From his first racing appearance in a DKW saloon it was evident that Scotsman Jim Clark had extraordinary talent. He dominated Formula Junior in the early part of the 1960 season, driving a Lotus, then was promoted to Formula 1 with Team Lotus in mid-season. Lack of a competitive engine in the Lotus held him back in 1961 but in 1962 he had the revolutionary monocoque Lotus 25 with the V8 Climax engine. His dominant successes with this car were the stuff of legend.

Clark had raced a D-type Jaguar at Spa in its 1958 sports-car meeting. That Archie Scott-Brown was killed in the race helped give Clark a lasting dislike of the circuit. Jim had engine problems during practice for the 1962 Belgian GP, so started well back on the grid. Despite his dislike of Spa he streaked past three cars in a single lap to take the lead and go on to a crushing win by nearly a minute. It was a double first: Clark's first Championship win and the first for the Lotus 25.

After practice problems with his gearbox in 1963, Clark was again well back on the grid. When the flag fell he made a superb start and passed everyone to take the lead by the time the cars had reached the crest of the

Eau Rouge hill. It was the last the field saw of him. Despite a thunderstorm soaking the track, he lapped the entire field. It was the first of seven wins that took him to a masterful World title in 1963.

By 1964 the Lotus 25 had lost its total dominance. Other teams were catching up. For the third year running Jim Clark had a poor practice for the Belgian GP Throughout the race he battled for second or third place. With his Lotus overheating, four laps from the finish he stopped to top up the header tank. At the start of the last lap he was fourth. During the lap two cars ahead of him ran out of fuel. Approaching the finish Clark was second, but Bruce McLaren's leading Cooper suffered total electric failure rounding the La Source Hairpin, in sight of the flag. Clark stormed down, passed the Cooper and took the flag for a lucky and unexpected victory.

A year later Clark had the Lotus 33-Climax, a refinement of the 25. This time he qualified on the front row. Heavy rain began to fall before the start and the treacherous circuit was awash. Graham Hill led at the start but Clark charged through Hill's spray on the Masta Straight to lead at the end of the first lap. Once again he dominated the race.

Jim Clark's 1965 mastery of the conditions on a circuit he hated was awesome. He lapped the whole field except Jackie Stewart and finished with a margin of almost a minute. It was the first of five consecutive wins that took him to his second World Championship. His drives at Spa confirmed the universal opinion that Clark was one of the all-time greats.

everywhere except the hairpin; when it was over, I was pleased.'

The Belgian Grand Prix continued at Spa until 1968, after which there was a year off while the start-line straight was widened and a wall built to separate the pits from the track. The race came back in 1970, but the now safety-conscious drivers did not like it. New purpose-built but anodyne Belgian circuits had opened at Nivelles and Zolder. After a year on the calendar the Grand Prix migrated in 1971. Formula 1 was lost to Spa for 11 years.

René Arnoux leads the field in his Ferrari 126C2B at the Bus Stop chicane during the opening lap of the 1983 Belgian Grand Prix.

Major international sports-car racing had returned in 1963 with a 500-km round of the World Sports Car Championship. It was run again in 1964 and 1965. In 1964 a 24-hour race for touring cars was promoted. This has since become a major fixture on the Spa calendar. The race is now regarded as the premier event for touring cars. The Sports Car Championship round was extended to a full 1,000km in 1966 and the race ran until 1975. Safety factors then intervened again, so it fell out of the Championship.

Compared with Spa, Zolder and Nivelles seemed little more than jumped-up go-kart tracks. The RACB realised that Spa needed to be updated, bringing it into line with the new safety regime initiated by Jackie Stewart and Swedish driver Jo Bonnier. The existing circuit was too long to be properly controlled. There was a new factor too: Formula 1 had become a hot television property. The TV world required shorter circuits.

A massive rebuild began in 1978. In all 4.3 miles (7.0km) was lopped off the old track. Malmedy, the Masta Straight and Stavelot were consigned to history. The gentle bends between Eau Rouge and Les Combes were replaced by a new Kemmel straight. A new section left the old course at Les Combes and ran across country, with sweeping curves through the forests. It rejoined the old course mid-way between Stavelot and La Source.

For Formula 1 the old pits were abandoned, replaced by a new pits/paddock complex immediately before the La Source hairpin, backing onto the old pits site. To slow the cars entering the new pit straight a controversial chicane, the Bus Stop, was

built on the bend where Seaman lost control in 1939. The lap distance of the new circuit was 4.3 miles (6.9km). Even with this drastic pruning it was still the longest World Championship circuit. To the great credit of its designers, the new section managed to maintain the magnificence and driving challenge of the old course while meeting modern needs.

A Ferrari takes the second Rivage corner during the 1993 Belgian Grand Prix.

The redesigned Spa was opened in 1979, and saw the return of the Belgian Grand Prix in 1983. After an interlude at Zolder the GP finally returned to its traditional Spa home in 1985.

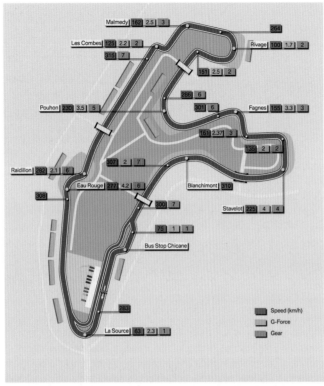

Malmedy | 162 | 2.5 | 3
264
Les Combes | 125 | 2.2 | 2
Rivage | 100 | 1.7 | 2
315 | 7
151 | 2.5 | 2
286 | 6
Pouhon | 230 | 3.5 | 5
301 | 6
Fagnes | 155 | 3.3 | 3
161 | 2.37 | 3
135 | 2 | 2
Raidillon | 262 | 2.1 | 6
307 | 2 | 7
Eau Rouge | 277 | 4.2 | 6
Blanchimont | 310
308
300 | 7
Stavelot | 225 | 4 | 4
75 | 1 | 1
Bus Stop Chicane
283
■ Speed (km/h)
■ G-Force
■ Gear
La Source | 63 | 2.3 | 1

Ralf Schumacher (Williams-BMW) locks a wheel while outbraking brother Michael's Ferrari in the 2000 Belgian Grand Prix.

The touring 24-hours was the first major event on the new circuit in 1979, followed by the 1,000km in 1982. Ironically it was safety which brought the Belgian Grand Prix back to Spa in 1983. A spate of accidents at Zolder put a question mark over the circuit. The new Spa circuit received general acclaim from the F1 drivers so, after another Zolder interlude, the Grand Prix came back to its traditional Spa home in 1985. It enabled Ayrton Senna to show his unique skills with four later consecutive wins from 1988 to 1991.

The Belgian Grand Prix at Spa has become a benchmark race in which the drivers can feel the hand of a more heroic past on their shoulders. A driver who can get results or even rapid laps feels he has shown the ultimate skills. One problem came with the revised format. Immediately after the start the field has to negotiate the La Source hairpin en masse. Several times this has brought grief to drivers, teams and especially to nose cones and front wings.

History was made in 1992 at Spa. In his first full Formula 1 season, new boy Michael Schumacher took the first of his record 91 World Championship victories in a Benetton. Despite the circuit changes, the weather factor at Spa still remains. Changeable conditions enabled Schumacher to show his mastery several times. He was able to dominate his rivals in the wet, sometimes on 'dry' tyres. He won the Belgian Grand Prix at Spa six times, an unequalled record.

Advertising issues forced a cancellation of the Grand Prix in 2003, while road works affecting access brought another cancellation in 2006. Back firmly in the Championship calendar, the 2008 Grand Prix saw controversy when Lewis Hamilton took the flag but was subsequently penalised for an incident at the Bus Stop chicane, giving victory to his Championship rival Felipe Massa.

Despite the 1978-79 changes, Spa ranks with Monza and Monaco as one of the few circuits which still maintain true links with the heroic Grand Prix races of the pre-World War 2 era. Best of all, among the multitude of artificial purpose-built circuits, enthusiasts and drivers alike still regard it as the supreme racing test.

Juan Pablo Montoya takes
La Source hairpin in his
McLaren-Mercedes MP4/20
during the 2005 Grand Prix.
He had a poor race, finishing
four laps behind.

Heikki Kovalainen takes his
McLaren-Mercedes MP4/24
over the brow at Eau Rouge
during the 2009 Grand Prix.

65

CHAPTER 8

Montlhéry

The 2.0-litre V12 Delage of Louis Wagner finishes second in the 1925 French Grand Prix behind the similar car of Robert Benoist.

THOUGH France was the birthplace of motor racing, after World War 1 other countries had stolen a march. France was almost alone in lacking a test track where continuous maximum speed could be maintained. Britain had Brooklands, the USA had Indianapolis and Italy had Monza. Even in defeated Germany there was the Avus.

Alexandre Lamblin, proprietor of the magazine *L'Aero Sport*, realised the need. He bought a 1,200 acre (486 hectare) farming estate 15 miles (24km) south-west of Paris between the towns of Linas and Arpajon, dominated by the Chateau of St. Eutrope. Lamblin instructed engineer Raymond Jamin to design a banked oval. Jamin produced a 1.57-mile (2.54-km) concrete bowl with two steep bankings, mounted on reinforced concrete pillars, joined by short straights. His design catered for a maximum speed of 145mph (230km/h).

Construction began on 15 March 1924 and was finished by September, a mere six months later. A grandstand seating 10,000 spectators was built from the timber of the trees felled for the circuit. On the infield was a row of permanent wooden pits. While the former chateau became a club house, workshops and garages were built under the bankings and leased to car manufacturers.

The first meeting was held on 11 and 12 October 1924 with races for cars and motorcycles. Reports spoke, perhaps optimistically, of 50,000 spectators. A strong British contingent appeared. The major race saw a fierce battle between Brooklands hero Parry Thomas with his Leyland-Thomas and Arthur Eldridge with the Fiat which had taken the Land Speed Record on the N20 road at nearby Arpajon the previous July.

Eldridge won and Thomas set the first lap record at 131.89mph (212.21km/h). The banked track was to become a magnet for record breakers. Before the end of 1924 a World 24-Hour record had been set by a Bignan.

In January 1925 a new venture began for which Lamblin had acquired some more land. An artificial road circuit was built. This joined up with the banked track, giving several alternative courses with the longest 7.67 miles (12.5km). The Automobile Club de France (ACF) chose the new circuit as its venue for the 1925 French Grand Prix. It was promoted as the centrepiece of a speed festival which had begun the previous weekend with races for motorcycles and cyclecars, followed by an 85-lap Touring Car Grand Prix. This attracted all the major

ROBERT BENOIST

sporting manufacturers but not the paying public, drawing a paltry 100 or so spectators.

Interest was greater in the Grand Prix. There was an impressive field of runners, but even this pulled in only some 25,000 customers, far fewer than expected. A 24-lap 1,000-km race, it began at 8:00am At first it was dominated by the all-conquering P2 Alfa Romeos. Then it rained, the course became slippery and Antonio Ascari in the leading Alfa was killed when he snagged palisades and overturned. The Alfa team was pulled out of the race and victory went to a Delage, to muted French satisfaction.

Montlhéry was being used almost daily for record attempts and testing. Between the World Wars record-breaking, even of minor class records, was a profitable business for owners and drivers. Oil companies and component manufacturers were happy to pay good bonuses for successes. These were advertised, often with suspect hyperbole. The more scheming would set a record which they knew they could beat, coming back soon afterward to raise the record and take more bonuses.

A Bentley broke the World 24-Hour record in September 1925. To gain maximum publicity, coinciding with the Paris Salon, a Panhard took the World Hour record at 115.3mph (185.5km/h). These records aroused intense rivalry between French manufacturers. Before the end of 1925 Renault and Voisin had both tried and failed to surpass the Bentley and

As winner of the European Championship in 1927, Robert Benoist was the forerunner of the present World Champions. Born in 1895, the son of a gamekeeper, the handsome hawk-nosed Benoist had been a fighter pilot in World War 1. He began racing with a 1.1-litre Salmson in 1922.

Benoist's skill in the spidery Salmson was noticed by manufacturer Louis Delage. In 1924 he drove a Delage in the French GP at Lyon, placing third. Moved to the newly-opened Montlhéry track in 1925, the Grand Prix was dominated in its early stages by the Italian P2 Alfa Romeos. When rain made the road slippery the leading Alfa of Antonio Ascari crashed, killing its driver. The other Alfas were withdrawn and a saddened and subdued crowd saw Benoist take the flag in his Delage.

Now leading the Delage team, Benoist had a difficult year in 1926, first of the new 1½-litre Grand Prix formula. The Delage was the fastest car but had problems, overheating its driver because the exhaust ran too close to his feet. In 1927 the revised Delage and Benoist were unbeatable. The combination ran away with the French GP at Montlhéry, finishing with a lead of 8 minutes, then went on to take the Spanish, Italian and British races. Robert was appointed to the Legion d'Honneur.

After Delage pulled out of racing at the end of 1927 Benoist withdrew to relative obscurity, managing a garage in Paris. Ettore Bugatti saw a talent going to waste so signed him up in 1934. Benoist tested cars and drove in some races. He was back at Montlhéry in 1935 for the French GP with an allegedly new Bugatti which turned out to be an amalgam of old parts.

In 1936, when France turned to sports-car racing. Robert Benoist was in the Bugatti team, leading at Montlhéry until his car went off tune and taking a second at Reims. His racing career ended in a blaze of glory in 1937 when he shared the winning Bugatti at Le Mans with Jean-Pierre Wimille. In a final interlude at Montlhéry he made an unsuccessful attempt to gain the 'Million' prize for Bugatti.

As a reservist, Benoist was called to the colours when World War 2 began. He had a dramatic escape from the advancing German army in 1940, using the performance of his road Bugatti to avoid capture. He came to England where he joined the SOE. Parachuted back into France, he organised a Resistance cell carrying out sabotage operations. He was captured by the Gestapo and escaped, but was recaptured. Despite horrific torture he gave nothing away. Benoist was hanged in Buchenwald concentration camp in 1944. Truly, a hero in peace and war.

Pierre de Vizcaya's T35 Bugatti leads the Delage of Robert Benoist in the 1925 French Grand Prix. Antonio Ascari is killed when his Alfa tangles with the fencing on this corner and overturns.

Garfield and Plessier take the World 24-hour record in this 9.0-litre Renault Type MC in May of 1925.

The Talbot of Albert Divo leads a thin field away at the start of the 1927 French Grand Prix. The eventual winner, Benoist (Delage), is in second place. The photographer is in pole position.

An unusual event had been organised in 1927: the *Journées Féminines*, a combined series of tests and short races for women drivers. It was run again in 1928 and 1929, attracting much attention as a social as well as a sporting event. In 1929 several drivers took part who made racing careers. The 1929 winner was 'Helle-Nice'. She competed against Lucy Schell who would be an important figure in French racing in the 1930s. Another competitor was the notorious Violette Morris, who would be executed by the Resistance for collaborating with the occupying Germans during the War.

The American Leon Duray was one of the more colourful racing characters of the 1920s. His real name was George Stewart but he felt the more flamboyant pseudonym would have greater appeal to race organisers. Driving Millers, Duray had many successes on US board tracks. In 1928 he set a lap record at Indianapolis which stood for nine years.

Duray brought two front-drive Miller 91s to Europe in 1929, with the aim of showing 'European racers were junk'. He didn't quite achieve it but he did show the amazing pace of his two cars. At Montlhéry, in his black overalls and helmet, he was soon called 'The Black Devil'. He brought out a Miller and set a five-mile record at 139.22mph (224.00km/h). After that he exchanged his Millers with Ettore Bugatti for three new 2.3-litre Bugattis plus a sum of money and went home.

Grand Prix racing had a massive resurgence in 1931. The French Grand Prix returned to Montlhéry. A 10-hour race, it was a three-cornered fight between Bugatti, Alfa Romeo and Maserati. To French delight a Bugatti shared by Louis Chiron and Achille Varzi came out on top.

Despite the relative success of the Grand Prix, there were problems. Montlhéry was losing money. Lamblin's dream had never been fully realised. He died in 1935 almost penniless. To help cash flow, the chateau was converted to a hotel. The British woman driver, Gwenda Stewart, took World and class records in the Derby-Miller, a Miller modified in the Derby works in Paris. She also took more records in a Morgan three-wheeler. Her efforts were recognised at the end of 1931 when she was awarded the Montlhéry Challenge Trophy.

In March of 1933 a remarkable record run began. A Citroën with a lightweight body, sponsored by the Yacco oil company, began a run which ended on 28 April. With the indefatigable 'Rosalie' the team of drivers took World records from 50,000 miles to 130,000km and from 18 to 54 days.

All record breaking came to a halt a few weeks later. There was a fire in one of the workshops beneath the banking. Several cars were burnt out while concrete piers carrying the track were destroyed, wrecking a section of the banking. The track was not reopened until the autumn, still with a roped-off

Panhard records. There was less racing in 1926 when the Grand Prix moved to the featureless banked Miramas track in Provence. The record breakers were still at it, Renault taking the 24 Hours and Panhard the Hour.

The Grand Prix returned in 1927 and Delage scored again. The winner was Robert Benoist who had also taken the 1925 race. With Grand Prix racing entering lean years, the race had only seven starters and a correspondingly small crowd. Hoping to match the success of Le Mans, a 24 Hour race was held in 1927. As at Le Mans it was a Bentley win, the first success for the legendary 4½-litre. The victors collected neither trophies nor prize money as the promoters were bankrupt!

This bankruptcy may have discouraged other promoters as there was little racing at Montlhéry in 1928 and 1929.

A trio of Salmsons heads the starters in the Grand Prix du UMF, a race for 1,100cc cars in 1927. Salmsons scored a 1-2 win.

The French Army supplies a light tank to recover the Napier-Railton after it crashes during a 24-hour record attempt in 1934.

'La Petite Rosalie 4' is the astonishing Citroën record-breaker which circulated Montlhéry for months in 1933.

hole in the banking. By December the track was in full working order. The Italian Amadeo Ruggieri came with a 5.0-litre V16 Maserati to attempt the World hour record. He lost control and was killed.

On 15 March 1933 the Citroën team came out again, this time with 'Rosalie IV'. They went on and on. By 27 July they had taken 106 World records up to 300,000km and 134 days. They paused in the middle of June because the French Grand Prix needed part of the banked track. With the run finished, Citroën put up a FFr 7 million stake for any manufacturer who could better 'Rosalie's' records. In mid-summer Gwenda Stewart pushed the outright track record to 145.9mph (234.81km/h).

Run over the combined circuit, the 1933 French GP was a battle between Italian cars driven by French and Italian drivers; Bugattis were nowhere. At the end it lay between Giuseppe Campari with a Maserati and Frenchman 'Phi-Phi' Etancelin in an Alfa. With two laps to go Campari made a stop for tyres and

Above: Rudi Caracciola (W25 Mercedes-Benz) applies opposite lock and Tazio Nuvolari (Tipo B Alfa) clips the verge during their battle in the 1935 French Grand Prix.

A Fiat Balilla leads a Simca-Fiat saloon, a Bugatti and an Aston Martin at the start of the 1939 Bol d'Or 24-hour race. The Aston Martin is the winner.

70

it looked like Etancelin's race. Then the Alfa's clutch jammed and Campari swept by to take his last win. He was killed at Monza three months later.

British driver John Cobb had commissioned the 24-litre Napier-Railton to dominate Brooklands and to break long-distance World records. It came to Montlhéry in April 1934 with the 24 Hour record as the target. During the night it skidded on the banking. It went to the top and slid broadside along the unguarded lip before ending up, badly bent, in the infield. Now in the Brooklands Museum, the great car still carries the scars on its frame. The accident showed that Montlhéry had the same problem as Brooklands: the faster cars had outgrown the track.

Traffic access was a constant problem from the outset at Montlhéry. For the 1934 French Grand Prix there were jams getting in and getting out. The draw was the Mercedes and Auto Union teams which had given racing a new and exciting face when the 750kg formula began. It wasn't a total French victory but a French driver, Louis Chiron, vanquished the German teams driving an Alfa Romeo.

The next year the pattern was established with a Mercedes 1-2 in 1935. A new French challenger, the SEFAC, never appeared, while an alleged new Bugatti turned out to be a revamped two-year-old car. After the Grand Prix, Gwenda Stewart brought out the Derby-Miller again and set a new lap record for the track at 147.79mph (237.79km/h). At the end of the run she lifted off too sharply and spun into the infield. Two wheels were torn off the car and she was badly bruised.

The ACF was unwilling to continue putting on races for German benefit, so in 1936 the French Grand Prix was run for sports cars. It was the main race in a French series throughout the season. It drew all the fastest sports cars in France, becoming a battle among Bugatti, Talbot-Lago and Delahaye. With a French win inevitable, a Bugatti came out on top. By 1936 there were fewer record attempts at Montlhéry. The surface of the banked track was deteriorating and the faster cars had outrun its limits.

The French Grand Prix came back in 1937. The Bugattis were withdrawn after practice and it was Talbot Lago against Delahaye. A Talbot won, driven by Chiron. The Bol d'Or, a somewhat bizarre race, had been held since the mid-1920s. It was a 24-hour event restricted to cars up to 1,100cc with the

A new Grand Prix Lago-Talbot receives its shake-down test at Montlhéry in 1950.

Georges Grignard shows a forceful style as he presses on to take his Lago-Talbot to victory in the 1950 Paris Grand Prix.

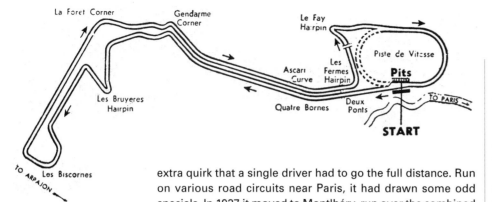

The Montlhéry circuit in 1954 from a contemporary diagram.

A Mercedes 300 alloy coupe is seen here on the Montlhéry banking.

extra quirk that a single driver had to go the full distance. Run on various road circuits near Paris, it had drawn some odd specials. In 1937 it moved to Montlhéry, run over the combined circuit with an abbreviated road section. The winner was a Chenard-Walcker driven by Charles Rigould who was described both as world weight-lifting champion and as the French all-in wrestling champion. Either way, a strong man.

With disappointment over the failure of France in Grand Prix racing, the 'Fonds des Course' was established. This was a government-run fund based on a driving-licence levy. The fund would give a big cheque to the manufacturer who was judged most likely to build a successful car. A 'Million Franc' competition was held at Montlhéry in 1937. A preliminary round in April had rigged rules to ensure that Bugatti had a slice of the fund. The main competition was held in August. On a day of high drama Bugatti and Delahaye went head to head. The Bugatti broke and Delahaye took the 'Million'. It made no difference; the German teams still won.

Montlhéry was gradually fading away. The Bol d'Or was held in 1938 and 1939 with wins for a Simca-Gordini and an Aston Martin. A 12-hour sports-car race went to a Talbot-Lago. In May 1939 the minor Coupe de Paris meeting drew the leading French drivers. Raymond Sommer took a Tipo 308 GP Alfa Romeo round the banked track, setting an all time record of 148.35mph (238.89km/h). Then came World War 2.

Montlhéry reopened in 1947. It had been a base successively for the French, German and American armies, but their depredations were patched up. A 12-hour sports-car race was held in 1948, witnessing an early Ferrari win. The following years brought many minor meetings. The Coupe de Salon at the end of the season drew most of the leading Grand Prix drivers. Although in a poor state, the banked track was still used for record runs, chiefly with production cars. The 24-hour Bol d'Or returned for several years, with greater sympathy allowing two drivers. In 1955 a 24-hour race for 2.0-litre sports cars was won by a Porsche.

The first race of a series, the 1,000km, was instituted in 1956. In its honour a row of concrete pits was built. Sadly there was a disastrous minor meeting at the end of 1956 when Louis Rosier, the former French Champion, was killed and the Swiss Benoit Musy met the same fate when his Maserati went over the top of the banking. As a repercussion of these accidents the 1,000km was not run again for four years. When it returned in

1960 it was promoted to be a round of the World Sports Car Championship. It remained in the racing calendar but was demoted to a lesser breed of race by the late 1960s. There was great French delight when a Matra scored in 1969 and 1970.

Two decades of minor races followed until, in 1994, the 1,000km returned. It enjoyed a French win for the turbocharged Venturi. The race came back again in 1995 but the track was in a bad state and the pits were dilapidated. It was the last major race at the historic track.

For some years Montlhéry hosted historic racing, then in 2005 it was closed. The future seemed bleak and demolition was threatened. In 2008 a ray of hope glimmered. It was announced that it would reopen for historic races and some renovation would be done. What the future holds for Montlhéry is uncertain, but the venue of so much history and drama should not be allowed to die.

The programme enlightened spectators of the 1970 1,000km de Paris.

The race-winning 917 Porsche of Derek Bell and Gijs van Lennep leads another 917 and a 512S Ferrari through a chicane during the 1971 1,000km de Paris.

CHAPTER 9

Pescara

With his remarkable twin-engined Tipo A Alfa Romeo, Giuseppe Campari dominates the 1931 Coppa Acerbo. He is leaving the start alongside a T51 Bugatti and a 26M Maserati.

ON a hot morning in August 1957 a dark-green car screamed along a long straight road beside the Adriatic Sea. The Vanwall flicked through two corners and was greeted by a waved chequered flag. The Italian dominance of World Championship F1 racing had ended. It was a unique day on three counts. The Pescara circuit had hosted a World Championship race for the only time. It was the longest circuit ever to be used for a Championship round. And after mixed messages in earlier races, it confirmed the arrival of British-green cars as a new force in Grand Prix racing.

In the early 1920s motor racing burgeoned in Italy. Many local clubs organised races on tough demanding road circuits. Among these was the AC di Pescara. Pescara was then a minor seaside resort, the principal town of the mountainous Abruzzo province.

The Auto Club chose a course which began with a long straight running along the Adriatic, going into the suburbs of Pescara. It turned right and climbed by a tortuous road into the mountains. At the top of the climb, in the village of Cappelle, it turned again, diving downhill on another straight and back to the seaside road. The distance was 15.85 miles (25.49km). By the standards of the time it was a relatively short circuit, but a tough one. The long coastal straight enabled cars to attain high speeds.

The first race over 10 laps in June 1924 wasn't a major event, though it had the impressive title of Coppa Acerbo. It was named after Tito Acerbo, who had been killed fighting with the Italian Army in 1918. His brother was the local Fascist political boss, which may have influenced the choice of title. The first Coppa was over ten laps of the stony, unmade roads.

The victor who received the gold Coppa was a young Alfa Romeo test driver, Enzo Ferrari. He and Alfa Romeo were struggling to build a reputation. Both would achieve it.

Recognising that it had a success on its hands, the Pescara club ran the Coppa again in 1926, this time over a testing 20 laps. The course was too much for the fastest car and driver, Emilio Materassi, who gave up after changing the shredded tyres of his Itala fourteen times in 16 laps. A 15-lap race for touring cars was run on the same day, the Targa Abruzzo. The name was perhaps influenced by the Targa Florio, as some observers likened the course to the legendary Sicilian track.

The Coppa/Targa races continued in the 1920s. Neither pulled in major fields, but big names appeared among the winners. Giuseppe Campari, the opera star-cum-racing ace, took the race in 1927 and 1928. In 1929 the meeting had dropped out of the calendar. The organisers realised that a new approach was needed. In 1930 the date was moved so the meeting coincided with the Ferragosto festival, the Feast of the Assumption, in mid-August.

Prima donna rivalry was a notable feature of Italian racing between the wars. Foremost was the bitter conflict between Achille Varzi and Tazio Nuvolari, both vying to be the leading national driver. It arose in 1928 when Varzi drove for a team organised by Nuvolari and considered he had been ripped off over car preparation and cost.

At the beginning of 1930 both men had been signed by Enzo Ferrari for his new Scuderia. Their antagonism came to a head at the beginning of August when ice-cold introvert Varzi walked out and signed with rival Maserati. To rub it in, he carried off the Coppa, sweeping past a fuming Nuvolari who lost time changing plugs on the mountain road. The race was gaining in stature as its guests of honour were Mussolini's sons Bruno and Vittorio.

Aiming to secure dominance in Grand Prix racing, in 1931 Alfa Romeo built a bizarre car as a back-up to its successful

Maseratis lead the field at the start of the 1,500cc Voiturette race in 1934. Hugh Hamilton, who goes on to win, has stalled his MG and is being push-started at the rear of the grid.

Luigi Fagioli takes the corner onto the main straight on his way to victory in the 1934 Coppa Acerbo with a W25 Mercedes.

Predominant at the start of the 1934 Targa Abruzzo are 8C 2300 and 8C 2600 Alfa Romeos. The race is a clean sweep for the Alfas entered by the Scuderia Ferrari.

Monza model. This 'Tipo A' had two engines mounted side-by-side in front of the driver who had to juggle with the tortuous manipulation of two linked gearboxes. Campari drove this monster and put it to good use, taking the Coppa. It was reported that on tight corners he stopped the inside engine, which aided cornering speed. Indicating the growing importance of the race, at the finish Campari was greeted by a minor royal, the Duke of Abruzzo, and trans-Atlantic air ace Marshal Balbo.

The Ferragosto had become a full motor-racing festival with the Coppa, the sports-car race and an additional Coppa for the 1,100cc voiturettes. Unfortunately the 1932 winner didn't get the gold Coppa as it was stolen a week before the race.

There was a small but significant landmark in 1933. The Anglo-American heir Whitney Straight had brought professional driving skills and preparation to his amateur team. He drove an MG in the 1933 *voiturette* race and won convincingly in a previous preserve of Italian and French machinery. The doubting organisers demanded stripping of the MG's engine after the race to verify the capacity. It was wholly legal and marked the beginning of British domination of the small-capacity racing classes.

The German teams came to Pescara in 1934. Leading the challenging Alfa Romeos was Algerian Guy Moll. Though only 24 he was showing outstanding talent. In the race Moll was lying second, biting away at the lead of the Mercedes in front. On the seaside straight, doing 160mph (260km/h), Moll's car was hit by a gust of wind and he went off the road, hitting the side of a house with tragic results.

The Coppa Acerbo was now a major Grand Prix fixture, so in 1934 the organisers raised their sights further. The Targa Abruzzo became a full 24-hour sports-car race, run during the weekend before the Coppa. It was run over 24-hours again in 1935. The voiturette race had also become a major event in a class which was rapidly gaining stature by 1935, having a full calendar of events throughout Europe. The races were mostly battles between Maserati and ERA. The rising British ace Richard Seaman won in 1935 with an ERA. He returned in 1936 to win again with a rejuvenated 1927 GP Delage, seeing off the modern rivals.

The speeds of Grand Prix cars had risen dramatically. In 1934, starting a trend which would become universal on racing circuits half a century later, a chicane was introduced at the end of the seaside straight just before the pits. Despite this, high speeds were still being recorded. Varzi had deserted Italian machines and gone to Auto Union on the principle, 'If you can't beat 'em, join 'em'. In 1936 he was timed at 183mph (295km/h).

Grand Prix racing had become the fiefdom of the German teams. It was hoped a change of formula in 1938 would redress the balance, but the dominance continued. The national and political prestige of Fascist Italy was at stake. In 1938 Alfa Romeo had produced the Tipo 158 which immediately set new standards in its 1,500cc class. It had been joined by a new and much more rapid Maserati. To cash in on this new supremacy, it was decided that in 1939 all former Grand Prix races in Italy would be run for 1,500cc cars.

The Coppa Acerbo was run under the new regime. It was an unhappy meeting. The leading motorcycle racer Giordano Aldrighetti, who had joined the Alfa team, was killed in a practice crash. In the race Catullo Lami was killed when he went off the road. It was an Alfa 1-2-3-4 after the works Maseratis — which had battled for the lead all the way — ran out of fuel on

Bernd Rosemeyer clips the kerb in Capelle village with his C-Type Auto Union on his way to a convincing victory in the 1936 Coppa Acerbo.

Tazio Nuvolari takes his D-type Auto Union into the winding uphill leg during the 1938 Coppa Acerbo, from which he retires early.

the last lap, just before the finish line. Italy entered World War 2 in June 1940 so there was no racing at Pescara for seven years. The war treated Pescara kindly. It fell to the British Eighth Army, advancing up Italy in June 1944. There was little active conflict in the region.

Racing returned to Pescara for the 1947 Ferragosto festival with no mention of the Coppa Acerbo. That title, with its Fascist undertones, had been conveniently forgotten. Now it was the Circuit of Pescara. Among the hordes of Fiat-based specials in

Manfred von Brauchitsch takes a narrow lead with his W154 Mercedes at the start of the 1938 Coppa Acerbo, ahead of his team-mate Hermann Lang and the Auto Union of Tazio Nuvolari.

the ambitious 20-lap sports-car race was a new machine, a Ferrari, which had made its debut at the beginning of the 1947 season. It went the distance, finishing second.

Pescara was a sports-car race again in 1948. This time victory went to rising star Alberto Ascari, with a Maserati. Four

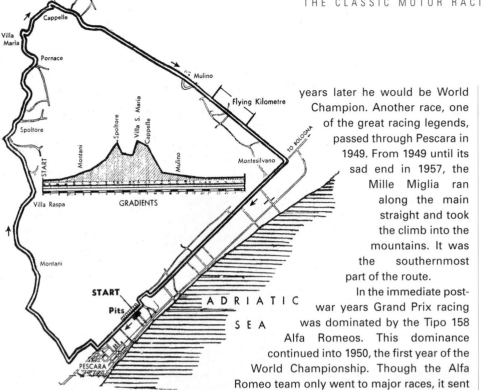

The circuit map Pescara circa 1955, also showing the gradient of the circuit.

years later he would be World Champion. Another race, one of the great racing legends, passed through Pescara in 1949. From 1949 until its sad end in 1957, the Mille Miglia ran along the main straight and took the climb into the mountains. It was the southernmost part of the route.

In the immediate post-war years Grand Prix racing was dominated by the Tipo 158 Alfa Romeos. This dominance continued into 1950, the first year of the World Championship. Though the Alfa Romeo team only went to major races, it sent two cars to Pescara in 1950 when Grand Prix racing came back to the circuit. It seemed the pair would have no opposition.

It was agreed before the race that Luigi Fagioli would lead the Alfas home. On the last lap, halfway down the main straight, the front suspension of Fagioli's car collapsed. His team-mate Fangio slowed to shepherd Fagioli to the line. Coming up behind the two Alfa hares was the tortoise Talbot-Lago of Louis Rosier. Fangio saw the looming Talbot and accelerated up the road to the flag just in time, while Fagioli limped home in third place. In practice Fangio had been timed at 192.84mph (310.08km/h).

It was like old times in 1951. The Alfas had met their match in the new unsupercharged 4½-litre Ferraris and stayed away, but the Ferraris came in force. The race went to the Argentine driver Froilan Gonzales, known affectionately as 'The Pampas Bull' for his physique and lurid driving style. Backing the Grand Prix event was a six-hour GT race which was a Lancia clean sweep.

For the next two years the Ferragosto festival was marked by 12-hour sports-car races. In 1953 the winning Ferrari was

Seen in Capelle village, Rudi Caracciola is on his way to an easy win with his W154 Mercedes-Benz in the 1938 Coppa Acerbo.

co-driven by Briton Mike Hawthorn whose talent had been recognised by Enzo Ferrari. The new 2½-litre formula brought back the Grand Prix cars in 1954, but it was a thin field and at the end only three Maseratis were running, a paltry spectacle on such a long circuit. The Le Mans disaster took its toll in 1955 when, along with most races in the calendar, the Pescara outing was cancelled.

In the middle of the 1957 season the FIA realised that it was running out of races to make a proper F1 World Championship. Several rounds had been cancelled. To make up the numbers it announced at short notice that the Gran Premio di Pescara would be a Championship round. The British Vanwalls had emerged as winning cars, taking their first victory in the British GP a month earlier. There were doubts about Vanwall reliability. Pescara would be Vanwall and Maserati head to head. Enzo Ferrari was having one of his regular quarrels with the Italian authorities so grudgingly sent one car.

To avoid the heat of the day the race began at 9:30am. The Ferrari driven by Luigi Musso led at the start, but after a lap Stirling Moss went to the front in the Vanwall. His pursuers never saw him again. Using the car's straight-line speed he pulled away. At the end of the 18 laps he was three minutes in front. The racing world had been shown the Vanwall had both speed and reliability. Moss said, 'Burning up those roads... It was a very exciting place.'

Formula 1 did not come to Pescara again. There was a gap of two years before the next race, now for the burgeoning Formula Junior. The winner in a Cooper, starting his international racing career, was a future Word Champion, New Zealander Denny Hulme.

It all came to an end in 1961. A four-hour sports-car race was the last on the circuit. Fittingly it was won by a Ferrari. Enzo had won the first race in 1924 and one of his cars won the last race.

Pescara had been a tough, unyielding circuit which demanded the best qualities in man and machine. The racing word was changing. The long heroic circuits had had their day. Like many others Pescara was consigned to the history books.

In one of the first races for the new marque, Franco Cortese takes a narrow lead with his Tipo 125S Ferrari at the start of the 1947 Circuito di Pescara. He finishes second.

Clemente Biondetti in a Tipo 166 Ferrari indicates to the driver of a Cisitalia that he should move over during the 1948 Circuito di Pescara.

STIRLING MOSS

Stirling Moss races through Capelle with his 250F Maserati during the 1954 Pescara Grand Prix. A broken oil pipe forces him out of the race when he has a commanding lead.

Stirling Moss.

Save for a season and a half interrupted by Mercedes-Benz, Italian cars ruled the roost in Grand Prix racing from the end of World War 2 until the mid-1950s. It was the avowed aim of British millionaire industrialist and racing enthusiast Tony Vandervell 'to beat those bloody red cars'. From 1954 Vandervell began developing his own Grand Prix car, the Vanwall. It was a slow climb from the back of the grid. His cars were fast, but they suffered many setbacks.

For 1956 he built a car which had the speed to beat the Ferraris and Maseratis, but it lacked reliability. Vandervell also needed a first-rank driver. Stirling Moss had hampered his early career by a patriotic desire to race British cars. Only when he drove for Maserati and Mercedes did he gain the successes his talent deserved. He drove a Vanwall to a minor win at Silverstone in 1956. For 1957 Moss threw his lot in with Vandervell to seek an all-British winning combination.

From the beginning of the 1957 season the Vanwall showed it was the fastest car on the circuits, albeit still plagued with minor reliability problems.

Triumph came at last in the British GP at Aintree, but the result was only achieved when Moss shared the winning car with Tony Brooks after his own car had failed and the opposition had dropped out. Worse still, in the next Championship round on the testing Nürburgring for the German GP, the Vanwalls had been woeful.

Tony Vandervell still craved the win that would show the Italian teams that his cars were indisputably the best. Though the Pescara Grand Prix appeared in 1957's World Championship calendar as a last-minute stop-gap, this didn't bother Vandervell. His cars were there. The long Pescara circuit climbed into the tortuous mountains, but the main straight beside the Adriatic suited the Vanwalls with their slippery aerodynamic shape.

Stirling Moss leaped into the lead at the start. The field, including 1957 World Champion Juan Fangio, never saw him again. Moss streaked away to win by a remarkable three minutes. Tony Vandervell was exultant. He and Moss had destroyed 'the bloody red cars' decisively and on their home ground. Moss and Vanwall started a run of success for British cars in Grand Prix racing which has continued ever since.

*Stirling Moss takes the
chequered flag in his
Vanwall in the 1957
Pescara Grand Prix.*

CHAPTER 10

Reims

The victorious Tipo B Alfa Romeo team rounds Thillois Hairpin in the 1932 French Grand Prix, Caracciola leading Borzacchini and Nuvolari. The circuit is then relatively undeveloped.

Between 1914 and 1918 the tides of war ebbed and flowed across the Champagne district of France east of Paris. The city of Reims was badly damaged. There was much devastation in the surrounding country. As France recovered from the war, motor racing revived and grew. Ambitious local clubs planned races, encouraged by local authorities that saw these as a chance to bring money into the locality. Among these was the Automobile Club du Champagne, based in Reims.

The club jumped on the motor-racing bandwagon in 1925. With sponsorship from a local newspaper, *L'Eclaireur de l'Est*, it promoted the grand-sounding Grand Prix de la Marne. This was held on a 13-mile (22km) circuit out on the rolling plains, east of Reims between the villages of Beine and Nauroy. With a motley field it was an unmemorable event. In 1926, however, the AC du C found a new circuit which was to become one of the all-time classics.

Sited about 4.5 miles (7km) west of Reims, it was triangular. The start/finish was on a straight between the villages of Thillois and Gueux. In Gueux it ran between the houses and turned right past a grocer's shop, climbing along fast bends through woods until it met the Reims-Soissons RN 31 road at La Garenne. Taking a right angle it followed a downhill straight until it met a sharp hairpin at Thillois, then back to the start.

In 1926 and 1927 Reims was still a minor event. The status was raised in 1928, when a 50-lap race pulled in better drivers. The winner in his first racing season was 'Phi-Phi' Etancelin. A wool merchant from Rouen, Etancelin drove his Bugatti to the circuits with his wife in the mechanic's seat. During the race she managed his pit. It was the start of a career which would cover nearly 30 years and culminate in the award of the Legion d'Honneur.

Next year Reims did even better with a remarkable 58 entries. Heading the field home by an amazing six-lap margin was Louis Chiron in a Bugatti. He would soon become one of the all-time Grand Prix stars. Key to the growing success of Reims was Raymond 'Toto' Roche, the moving force behind its organisation. Though regarded by some as a comic character, Roche was guiding the Reims circuit to greatness.

The Marne GP was continuing to grow in importance. By 1930 many of the major teams and drivers were competing and *L'Eclaireur de l'Est* was still providing sponsorship. At the end of the 1931 race the drivers went to a champagne party in the pits. At that time, to be classified as a finisher a driver had to complete the full distance. Back markers, struggling to the flag, had the frustration of watching more successful rivals quaffing happily, while hoping the champagne would still be flowing when they finished.

Reims arrived at the top level in 1932, when it was chosen to host the French Grand Prix. It was a round of the European Championship, a forerunner of the present World Championship. To mark the occasion new concrete pits and a huge grandstand were built. The five-hour race was dominated by the team of Tipo B Alfa Romeos.

It was evident that there was rivalry between the drivers. Nuvolari expected to be Champion. It seems a Reims win for him had been agreed by the team. His team-mate Rudi Caracciola took the lead against team orders so Nuvolari passed him amid much fist-shaking. Vittorio Jano, the designer

Left: *In a duel of Tipo B Alfa Romeos Louis Chiron leads Achille Varzi and Guy Moll on the opening lap of the 1934 Grand Prix de la Marne. Chiron wins ahead of Moll.*

and team manager, wanted a showpiece 1-2-3 at the finish but Nuvolari would have none of it, not trusting his team-mates, and kept a safe distance ahead at the flag.

The 1933 GP saw a finish for which Reims would become famed. It was back to the Marne GP over 50 laps, which enjoyed a duel among the Monza Alfa Romeos of Etancelin, Guy Moll and Jean-Pierre Wimille. With two laps to go Moll stopped for fuel, but as Etancelin and Wimille came out of the Thillois hairpin for the last time, their cars were almost abreast. Etancelin won the acceleration dash to the line by one-fifth of a second.

By 1935 the arrival of the German teams in Grand Prix racing had created two divisions of racing. In the premiership were those races in which the German teams appeared. The rest were in division two. Reims was among the lower orders. Two Auto Unions were promised but withdrawn. Run in two heats and a final, the Marne GP was backed by a 28-lap GP de Tourisme for sports cars. It was a foretaste of things to come with a Delahaye victory.

Taking third place in the 3.0-litre class was Jean Desvignes in a Bugatti. After the race Desvignes set off to drive back to Paris. About five miles from the circuit on the RN31, Desvignes swerved to avoid an oncoming car and was killed when his Bugatti hit a tree.

Unable to beat the Germans, in 1936 French race organisers followed the lead from the Automobile Club de France. The French Grand Prix was run for the new generation of powerful French sports-racing cars so most major races in France followed suit. The Marne GP was a three-cornered fight among Bugatti, Delahaye and Talbot-Lago. After a fierce race Bugattis finished 1-2-4. Running at the rear of the field to win the 3.0-litre class was an SS100 Jaguar. It was the first international success for a company which would have a huge impact on the sport two decades later.

Sports-racing cars were back again in 1937. This time Bugatti sent a thinly disguised Grand Prix T59. It ran away with

the race and there was dark talk of illegal fuel, but Ettore Bugatti was held in such awe and reverence that there was no investigation.

The French Grand Prix returned, run for Grand Prix cars again in 1938. The Gueux-La Garenne-Thillois sections had been widened. The race was almost a farce. Only nine cars started and after two laps only five were left. At the end there were four runners capped by a Mercedes triumph. There was

Manfred von Brauchitsch leads Mercedes-Benz team-mate Hermann Lang at the start of the 1938 French Grand Prix. The front rows are dominated by the German teams, with also-ran French Lago-Talbots, SEFAC and Bugatti at the back.

An impressively big chequered flag is waved at Manfred von Brauchitsch as he wins the 1938 French Grand Prix in a W154 Mercedes-Benz.

The team of D-type Auto Unions lines up in front of the Reims pits before the 1939 French Grand Prix.

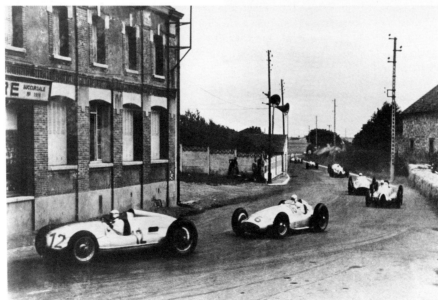

Hermann-Paul Müller's D-Type Auto Union leads Rudi Caracciola's W154 Mercedes-Benz at Gueux on the opening lap of the 1939 French Grand Prix. Caracciola crashes before the end of the lap and Müller goes on to win.

*Hermann Müller makes a
pit stop with his D-type
Auto Union at half-distance
in the 1939 French Grand
Prix. He carried on to victory.*

Mike Hawthorn's F2 Ferrari 500 just heads Juan Manuel Fangio's Maserati A6GCM in the dash to the flag at the end of their legendary duel in the 1953 French Grand Prix.

Swiss Armand Hug rounds Thillois Hairpin, heading for an easy win with his Maserati 4CM in the 1939 1,500cc voiturette race.

En route to victory, French veteran Louis Chiron takes his Lago-Talbot down the long tree-lined straight to Thillois in the 1949 French Grand Prix.

a better field in 1939, but the Mercedes team was off-colour with carburetion ailments. All three dropped out so the bitter rival Auto Union took the honours.

Unlike events 25 years earlier, World War 2 left Reims and its circuit virtually unscathed. Racing returned to Reims in 1947. Grand Prix racing was dominated by the Tipo 158 Alfas but these didn't run so the best of the rest fought it out. In 1948 the Alfas were there for the French GP They ran true to form with a 1-2-3. For a few laps a very sick and ailing Nuvolari took over a Maserati. It was his last Grand Prix drive. Driving a Gordini, Juan Fangio witnessed this degrading exploitation of Nuvolari and vowed never to be in a similar position.

In 1949 there were two French GPs. One was held at Reims and to huge French delight it brought a win for Chiron's Talbot-Lago. It was his last win; the old brigade was fading away.

When the World Championship began in 1950, the nature of Grand Prix racing changed for ever. While Championship rounds were the races which mattered, the rest were minor happenings, gradually dropping from the calendar. The Alfas returned, crushing the Reims field with a three-lap margin at the end.

It was a different story in 1951, when Alfa's dominance was being challenged and would soon be ended by Ferrari. It was an Alfa win, only gained by putting team leader Fangio into the car of the team's number three, Fagioli, in mid-race. A small piece of history was made. At 52, sharing the victorious car made Fagioli the oldest driver ever to win a Championship round. This cut little ice with the choleric Fagioli, who was outraged at having been asked to relinquish his Alfa.

At the end of 1951 huge changes were made to the Reims circuit, triggered in part by the rivalry with Spa for the claim to be the fastest European circuit. Also a circuit which only used public roads was no longer able to meet the demands of modern racing. A new road was built that cut across country with a very fast bend immediately after the start. With fast left and right hand curves, it joined the RN31 with a hairpin at Muizon. This gave a longer dash along the RN31 down to Thillois. Thillois was rounded off to give a faster exit to the finish.

Gueux village and the wooded back leg to La Garenne were abandoned. This created a 5.2-mile (8.35km) circuit with two flat-out sections joined by hairpins. Greatly improved, the facilities were at that time probably the best in Europe. A resident flock of sheep was engaged to keep down the grass in the public enclosures.

In 1952 and 1953 the World Championship was contested by 2.0-litre F2 cars. The French GP went to

A contemporary ciruit map of Reims in 1954.

Fangio in a Mercedes-Benz W196 leads team-mate Karl Kling under the Dunlop Bridge on the main straight during the 1954 French Grand Prix. The race marks the reappearance of the three-pointed star in Grand Prix racing after a 15-year hiatus.

Alberto Ascari, unfamiliar in a Maserati 250F, retires with a burst engine at the end of the first lap of the 1954 French Grand Prix

Rouen in 1952, but Reims hosted a round in the season-long race series, the Grands Prix de France. All the Grand Prix teams attended. To huge French joy the three-hour race was won by a Gordini driven by Jean Behra, beating the all-conquering Ferraris. It was murmured that perhaps the Gordini had an over-sized engine, but amid the euphoria the Reims officials didn't look too closely. In 1952 the British Jaguar team had failed dismally at Le Mans, so a win for Stirling Moss in a 50-lap sports-car curtain-raiser gave the team fresh hope.

The 1953 French GP at Reims has become a motor-racing legend. A multi-car slipstreaming battle ended with a head-to-head between Juan Fangio and British new boy Mike Hawthorn. Hawthorn took the race by two lengths.

History was made again in 1954. After 15 years Mercedes returned to the Grand Prix world, Reims chosen for the debut. The streamlined silver cars swept the red and blue opposition aside, returning to their former supremacy. The Grand Prix was preceded by a 12-hour sports-car race which began at midnight. British enthusiasts were heartened when it ended with a Jaguar 1-2-3-4. During the 12 hours the rising sun in the morning could dazzle drivers approaching Thillois. To block this a screen was hung from the pedestrian bridge before the corner.

After the 1955 Le Mans disaster motor racing came to a stop in France, including Reims. Ferraris won in 1956, 1957 and 1958. In 1956 it was the French GP In 1957 the national Grand Prix went to Rouen but the F1 cars came for the Grand Prix de Reims.

In 1958 Hawthorn took the win in the Grand Prix on his way to be the first British World Champion. It was a muted win as his team-mate Luigi Musso, who had won the 1957 race, was killed when he left the road on the super-fast bend after the pits, one of several drivers claimed by this bend. In fourth place, nursing home a Maserati with a slipping clutch, was Juan Fangio, driving his last race.

Reims witnessed yet another Ferrari win in 1959. By now the engine in F1 cars was living behind the driver, but Enzo Ferrari was bucking the trend. Briton Tony Brooks, who won the Grand Prix, was one of the last drivers to prevail in a front-engined car.

Against an increasing dominance of British green, Ferrari made a comeback in 1961 for the first year of the 1½-litre formula. A full team of Ferraris came to Reims to fight the British and an extra Ferrari was sent for new boy Giancarlo Baghetti driving in his first Championship round. It was the usual slipstream fight and for once the Ferraris wilted. Baghetti alone was left to carry on the battle. At the end he won a dash from Thillois to the line to become the only driver to win on his Championship driving debut. The French GP came back to Reims in 1963 and 1966. The circuit was facing competition from other venues anxious to stage an increasingly prestigious and profitable race with the new benefit of TV revenues.

In 1963 Jim Clark, the outstanding talent in a new generation, took the flag in a Lotus. Then came the last Grand Prix on the circuit in 1966. It saw veteran Jack Brabham, who

Seen at Reims in 1957 with Maurice Trintignant, Ferrari's Dino V6 made its debut at 1.5-litre capacity in a front-engined monoposto.

MIKE HAWTHORN

Tall, tow-headed Mike Hawthorn exploded onto the British racing scene. Driving Riley sports cars he scored a string of wins in 1951. He moved up into the Grand Prix world in 1952 when the 2.0-litre Formula 2 became the World Championship category. Though his Cooper-Bristol was outclassed by the Italian teams, he picked up some impressive places. In spite of its lack of top speed the Cooper took him to seventh place on his first appearance at Reims.

Enzo Ferrari spotted his talent and signed up Hawthorn for 1953, a season when Ferrari and Maserati were neck and neck for top honours. From the start at Reims that year the four cars of each team began a slipstreaming battle. At half distance the race was led by veteran Juan Fangio on Maserati and relative rookie Hawthorn. The pair swapped the lead several times each lap.

With two laps to go, Hawthorn realised that Fangio's Maserati had lost first gear, vital for acceleration out of the crucial Thillois Hairpin. On the last lap Hawthorn came out of Thillois and went for the line, getting about two lengths' advantage. Holding this to the line, the bow-tied Briton was acclaimed the winner of the French GP. If not the greatest Grand Prix ever, as some said at the time, it was certainly one of the most exciting. Hawthorn made only one mistake that memorable day. At the after-race party he dallied intimately with the secretary of 'Toto' Roche, the race organiser. She subsequently had a son.

For several years Mike Hawthorn had mixed fortunes in his racing career. In 1956 he took second place in the Reims 12 Hour sports-car race with a D-type Jaguar. In 1958 he was back with Ferrari and a strong contender for the World Championship. With the fastest car in the French GP, the 246 Dino, Hawthorn led from flag to flag.

Mike's old adversary Fangio was driving a Maserati in what turned out to be his final race. Hawthorn came up to lap him but eased off to show respect for the great Argentinean. It was a sad race for Ferrari and Hawthorn, as his team-mate Luigi Musso went off the road and was killed.

The Reims race was Hawthorn's only Championship win of the 1958 season. That, with his other results, secured him the World title. He didn't live long to enjoy it. Hawthorn was killed in a road accident a few months later.

At the start of the 1959 Formula 2 race, Stirling Moss's Cooper-Borgward is flanked by the Porsches of Hans Hermann and Jo Bonnier. Moss scored a convincing win.

had won in 1960 with a Cooper, take the flag in one of his own cars on his way to a third World Championship.

The 12 Hours had continued, seeing many Ferrari wins. In 1967 the Ferrari sequence was broken by a Ford victory with a GT40. After the circuit revision in 1952 speeds had been rising constantly. In 1959 Brooks's winning average was 125.45mph (205.07km/h). In the last Grand Prix in 1966, Brabham pushed the average up to 135.05mph (217.35km/h). The fastest lap of all came in the 1967 12-Hours — 142.32mph (229.04km/h) by a Lola-Chevrolet.

Although Formula 1 visited Reims no more after 1966, the active Formula 2 circus returned for several seasons. This brought all the leading drivers; once again the circuit saw hectic slipstreaming. It was also a venue for Formula Junior and Formula 3. The last Formula 2 race in 1969 was fittingly won by Frenchman François Cévert.

Racing at Reims ended in 1970. The organisers had financial problems. More significantly, there were increasing difficulties in closing the RN31 with the consequent traffic disruption. Enthusiasts still make pilgrimages to the circuit where the huge grandstands and the pits are a reminder of the heroic races once witnessed by enthralled crowds fuelled by the region's sparkling beverage.

The might of Scuderia Ferrari monopolises the front row in the 1961 French Grand Prix with its Dino 156 F1. Phil Hill (16) goes on to the 1961 World Championship.

Cliff Allison's Ferrari Dino 156 leads the Porsche RSK of Jo Bonnier in the 1959 Formula 2 race. Allison's engine broke and Bonnier was third.

CHAPTER 11

Mille Miglia

The first Mille Miglia winner is the OM of Nando Minoia and Morandi in the 1927 race. They're climbing the Raticosa Pass where the road is rough and tough.

Above right: **Rudi Caracciola wins the 1931 race in an SSKL Mercedes-Benz. He is the only German driver to gain a Mille Miglia victory.**

IN 1926 four rich and influential Italian racing enthusiasts began significant discussions. They wanted to see an Italian race which would gain the importance that the Le Mans 24-Hours had already achieved. They met in Brescia, their home city on the northern Italian plains near Lake Garda. Count Aymo Maggi and Franco Mazzotti had raced Bugattis. Renzo Castagneto was secretary of the AC di Brescia and Giovanni Canestrini was an influential motoring journalist.

At first the idea was a race from Brescia to Rome but Mazzotti, perhaps influenced by a visit to the USA, suggested it should be over a distance of 1,000 miles (1,600km). The 'Mille Miglia' distance was also one thousand of the ancient Roman miles, giving undertones of the earlier heritage — an influence much approved by Italy's Fascist leaders. Mazzotti's suggestion was accepted and concurrence came from the Royal Automobile Club of Italy on 2 February 1927. It was a hark-back to the heroic open-road racing of the early days, reviving memories of the Paris-Bordeaux and Paris-Vienna.

A figure-of-eight course was chosen. It ran south from Brescia to Bologna, thence via Florence to Rome. Crossing the Apennines to the Adriatic at Ancona, it ran north back to Bologna. Then it ran north-east via Padua to Feltre on the edge of the Dolomite mountains before returning to Brescia. The roads for much of the distance were poor. Crowd control was minimal.

Though it could have been a disaster, the first Mille Miglia on 26 and 27 March 1927 was a huge success. Seventy-seven cars started at one-minute intervals, mostly Italian with a smattering of French machines. The race began at 8:00am with the largest cars leaving Brescia first. The first to leave Brescia, starting a heroic and legendary tradition, was an Isotta-Fraschini driven by Aymo Maggi. The co-driver was Bindo Maserati, one of the car-building brothers.

When the field reached Rome it was led by an Alfa Romeo that expired soon afterwards, originating the long-standing tradition that the car which led at Rome never won. Twenty-one hours after the start in the early light, the winning car was back at Brescia, an OM driven by Nando Minoia. He was followed by two more OMs and a pair of Lancias. Maggi's Isotta came sixth. Fifty-four cars finished the course. Astonishingly the race was blessed by no major accidents.

The Mille Miglia was run again in 1928. Its reputation was spreading. Ettore Bugatti entered a team of three cars with Italian drivers, led by Tazio Nuvolari. The Bugattis ran against a new generation of 6C Alfa Romeos. In the mountains the Alfas proved more nimble than the Bugattis with

1927-1930

Start & Finish
Brescia
Padua
Mantua
Parma
Bologna
Pesaro
Siena
Perugia
Rome

victory going to an Alfa driven by burly racer-cum-opera singer Giuseppe Campari.

The race became an Alfa fiefdom; Campari took the honours again in 1929 and Nuvolari, back in an Alfa, won in 1930. It became another stage for Nuvolari's bitter feud with fellow Italian Achille Varzi. He had left the Brescia start after Varzi. There is a story, perhaps apocryphal, that when he was catching Varzi on the road in the latter stages of the race, he switched off his lamps to prevent Varzi knowing he was close behind, relying on Varzi's lamps to show him the way.

The Italian racing community happily expected that 'their' Mille Miglia would be the playground of local drivers, familiar with the circuit. These expectations were rudely shattered in 1931. German ace Rudi Caracciola arrived with a 7.1-litre SSKL Mercedes and proceeded to lead the Italians home, winning by a margin of 11 minutes. During his career Caracciola scored countless wins and was regarded by many as the top driver in Grand Prix racing during the 1930s. His Mille Miglia win was among his greatest drives.

There were very slight variations to the route in 1931 and the revised course was used in 1932 and 1933. The Italian domination resumed, Alfas took the first seven places in 1932, going even better

with the first ten spots in 1933. In 1933 a minor British success fell to a team of K3 MGs in the 1,100cc class, taking both class and team prizes.

Another course revision in 1934 cut out Feltre. The course ran from Padua to Treviso with a detour into the outskirts of Venice. None of this stopped the Alfa domination, Nuvolari won in 1933, but Varzi had his revenge with victory in 1934. In the minor classes the Italian cars held sway. Maserati, Lancia and Fiat were sharing the spoils, so surprise accompanied Aston Martin's win in the 1,500cc class in 1935.

The entry list peaked in 1930 with 135 starters. After that it tailed off, but 124 came to the Brescia start in 1937. For the first time since 1931 the Alfas were challenged. A French Delahaye came third. The following year saw the first major revision to the course. Instead of following the inland route from Florence to Rome via Siena, it deviated west from Florence to the Mediterranean coast. Cars passed through Pisa then ran down the coast to Rome before joining the usual run back to Brescia via Bologna.

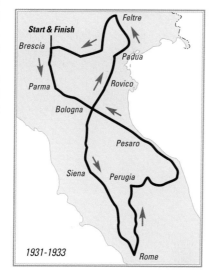

1931-1933

Start & Finish
Brescia
Treviso
Rovico
Piacenza
Parma
Bologna
Pesaro
Siena
Perugia
1934-1937
Rome

Every year average speeds were rising. In 1927 Minoia's OM had averaged 47.95mph (77.23km/h). By 1938 the victorious 2900C Alfa of Clemente Biondetti was back in Brescia after only 11 hours on the open road for an average of 84.07mph (135.39km/h). The race was drawing more foreign entries. A Delahaye was fourth and a Lago-Talbot fifth in 1938, while the 2.0-litre class was a clean sweep for a team of BMW 328s. On the return leg to Brescia in 1938, a Lancia spun on tram lines in Bologna and ran into the spectators. Ten were killed, including seven children, and another 23 were badly hurt.

As a consequence of the accident the Mille Miglia was not held in 1939. In April 1940 Europe was at war. Italy was still neutral, so the Mille Miglia was held again but in a new format. It was run over a 103-mile (167km) triangular circuit from Brescia to Cremona, on to Mantua, then back to Brescia. It was called the Gran Premio di Brescia delle Mille Miglia. The competitors had to cover nine laps of the circuit so the traditional distance remained.

Although Germany, Britain and France were at war, a team of BMWs was sent to Brescia. From France came a team of Delages. During the formalities before and after the race neither team acknowledged the existence of the other. History was made. Enzo Ferrari had broken

Nuvolari's Ferrari 166 SC falls to bits during his fruitless pursuit of victory in the 1948 race.

away from Alfa Romeo with high drama. He was barred legally from racing cars with his name, but two Fiat-based cars were built by his 'Auto-Avio Costruzioni' and entered as '815's. It was the start of an incredible chapter of motor racing history. The race was a battle between the BMWs and Alfas and the BMWs finished victorious. Two months later Italy entered the war.

Although Italy was a battleground between 1943 and 1945 as the British and American armies fought northwards, Italian motor racing was quick to recover once the war ended. Three of the original organisers of the race put it on again in its original format. The fourth, Franco Mazzotti, had been killed in action in 1943, flying with the Regia Aeronautica.

The first post-war Mille Miglia was run on 21 June 1947. It had been intended to run it in April but road repairs caused a postponement. A new route was chosen. Running east from Brescia to Padua, it turned south and ran parallel with the Adriatic as far as Fano. Then it turned west crossing the Apennines via Spoleto to Rome. Running up the Mediterranean coast to Livorno, it turned inland to Florence and thence to Bologna. There was then a long westerly run as far as Turin before turning east again to return to Brescia via Milan.

Start & Finish
Brescia
Treviso
Piacenza
Rovico
Parma
Bologna
Pisa
Pesaro
Livorna
Grosseto
Spoleto
1938
Rome

Despite shortages of fuel and tyres there were 155 starters, with hordes of Fiats and Lancias in the touring classes. With a change of tradition the fastest cars started at the rear of the field. The race became a battle of the old and new. Clemente Biondetti won in a pre-war Alfa Romeo coupé, but was fought all the way by Nuvolari in an 1.1-litre Fiat-based Cisitalia, a new post-war marque.

Biondetti was back again in 1948 and won this time with a Ferrari. Nuvolari, now sick with emphysema, was also in a Ferrari, putting up a valiant fight until he flagged and the car fell apart. New marques were appearing from other countries. A British Healey won one of the touring classes.

The Biondetti/Ferrari combination triumphed again in 1949, this time racing over another course variation. It ran anti-clockwise from Brescia to Parma, then down the west coast to Rome. Crossing the Apennines to Pescara, it went up the east-coast road as far as Ravenna and thence via Padua and Verona back to Brescia. As usual the drivers faced every kind of weather. In the mountains they contended with mist and low cloud as well as the tortuous and testing roads. There was another change in 1949. The cars were given a race number

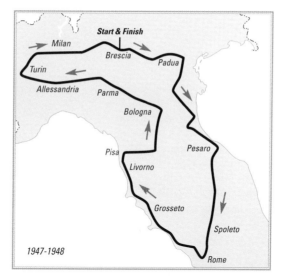

1947-1948

*Far left: **Giovanni Bracco** passes through Rome on his way to victory with a Ferrari 250S in 1952. The race is run in almost continuous rain.*

A typical British private entry, the HWM-Jaguar of George Abecassis waits on the starting ramp in 1954. The navigator is Denis Jenkinson, who partnered Moss in his 1955 victory.

Alberto Ascari has a solo drive to win the 1954 race with a Lancia D24.

The Mille Miglia was not always about brutal sports-racing cars and stylish GTs. Mario Cipollo finishes in 267th place with his Isetta in 1955.

Bottom right: **The Mille Miglia always produced notable drives. Francesco Giardini finished fourth overall and won the 2.0-litre class with his Maserati A6GCS/2000 in 1955.**

which was the time they left the start at Brescia. Spectators could see immediately who was doing well, progressing up the field.

There was a strong foreign challenge in 1950. A team of British XK120 Jaguars was entered, one driven by none other than Biondetti. The Jaguars were delayed by minor problems but finished fifth and eighth. The race went to the Ferrari of Giannino Marzotto, one of four motor-racing brothers. The Fratelli Marzotto were rich textile manufacturers. Yet again the route changed. It was run clockwise on much the same course as 1949 but with a detour through Florence and Bologna on the return leg. This took the cars through Modena, the Maserati and Ferrari home.

It was a tradition of the Mille Miglia that unlikely cars would produce remarkable results. In 1951, once again, the Jaguars fell by the wayside. Victory went to a Ferrari in the hands of Maserati and Ferrari ace Luigi Villoresi, but it was close. Placing second was a touring Lancia Aurelia driven by Giovanni Bracco. At the finish the fiery Bracco received a bigger ovation than the winner.

Mercedes-Benz had come back to motor racing in 1952. A team of formidable 300SL coupés made its first appearance in the Mille Miglia, a race greatly esteemed by the Germans. In a race run in rain throughout Giovanni Bracco took the honours for Ferrari but the 300SLs, perhaps better suited to the conditions, were second and fourth. In the fourth-placed car was Rudi Caracciola, returning to the Mille Miglia after a 21-year break. The race was now pulling in huge fields. There were 501 starters, mostly Italian amateurs.

In 1952 the course changed again to a route it would keep until the end of the series. It ran from Brescia to Padua, down the coast to Pescara. The usual run over the mountains to Rome continued up the middle of Italy through Florence to Bologna and via Piacenza to Brescia.

In 1953, with the race becoming a round in the new World Sports Car Championship, the home teams faced challengers. From Britain came Aston Martin and Jaguar. France sent Gordini. Giannino Marzotto won again with a Ferrari. In second place with a remarkable drive was Juan Fangio with an Alfa Romeo. For most of the return leg he only had effective steering on one front wheel. Belgian journalist Paul Frère won the unlimited touring class in an unlikely 5.3-litre Chrysler Saratoga saloon. Apart from an Aston Martin's fifth place, the other foreign challenges faded away.

The race had dramatic farce. Film director Roberto Rossellini drove a Ferrari. Having recently married film star Ingrid Bergman, he raced against her wishes. At Rome she flung herself across the car and refused to move until he agreed to withdraw.

For many years Lancia had watched Ferrari and Maserati scoop international racing honours. To redress the balance, Lancia entered top-level racing in 1954. A 3.3-litre D24 Lancia won, driven by World Champion Alberto Ascari. Unlike most drivers, Ascari elected to go the distance without a co-driver or passenger. In second place was the Ferrari of another Marzotto, brother Vittorio. Nuvolari had died in 1953, so in 1954 the course detoured through Mantua, his home town, in homage to a magnificent driver.

Mercedes returned to Grand Prix racing in 1954. In 1955 the German team produced the 300SLR, a sports-car derivative of their Grand Prix machine. In one of the 300SLRs was Stirling Moss, the British ace, the greatest driver in the modern era

CLEMENTE BIONDETTI

THE daunting Mille Miglia inspired many legendary drives. The exploits of Rudi Caracciola and Stirling Moss are renowned. In Italian eyes one driver stands above all others. Clemente Biondetti's record in the race was unrivalled.

Born in 1898 to a humble Sardinian family, Biondetti began motorcycle racing in 1923, then turned to cars. Starting with a Salmson, he moved on to a Bugatti. Then in 1931 the Maserati brothers offered him the post of a works driver. Continuing to race into the 1930s with a variety of cars, he became a member of Scuderia Ferrari, the Alfa Romeo works team, in 1935. Little success came as the Alfas were mere noises off to the German teams.

It came good for Biondetti in 1938. Driving one of the magnificent 2900C Alfa sports cars, he won the Mille Miglia. He also drove the new Tipo 158 voiturette, taking it to a second place on its debut at Livorno. There was no Mille Miglia in 1939, but Biondetti continued in the Tipo 158 and beat the best of the Italian drivers at Pescara. He finished fourth in the restricted 1940 Mille Miglia, then suffered inactivity until racing began again after World War 2.

Now coming up to 50 years old, Biondetti was back in a 2900C Alfa for the 1947 Mille Miglia, in which he took the honours. Having driven for the Scuderia Ferrari in the 1930s, Biondetti was among the first Ferrari drivers when Enzo's creations burst onto the racing world.

A Ferrari coupé took Clemente to victory in the 1948 Mille Miglia. He backed this with victory in the first post-war Targa Florio. Competing against drivers young enough to be his sons, in 1949 Biondetti scored a Mille Miglia hat trick with one of the legendary Ferrari barchettas and also took the Targa Florio again.

Jaguar recognised the value of Clemente Biondetti's experience. He drove the British marque in the 1950 Mille Miglia and at Le Mans in 1951. Though the years were beginning to tell and in failing health, Biondetti took the flag in the 1953 Bari Six Hours. His swan song came in the 1954 Mille Miglia with a fourth place for Ferrari; he was lifted exhausted from the car at the finish.

By now Biondetti was suffering from cancer. He faded rapidly, dying early in 1955. A remarkable man, Clemente Biondetti scored his major victories at an age when most drivers had already retired from the sport.

Both the man and his cars have an honoured place in Italian motor racing.

---

never to be World Champion. Moss had as his companion writer and motorcycle racer Denis Jenkinson who had already been a passenger to the World Sidecar champion. Using a system of course notes to put Moss on level terms with the locals, the pair triumphed. It was only the second win by a non-Italian driver and car. Moss's average was 97.90mph (157.65km/h). Setting a record which was never broken, Moss took a mere 10 hours 7 minutes to cover the course. It was the greatest drive of Moss's career.

The 1956 Mille Miglia saw Eugenio Castellotti lead home a Ferrari 1-2-3-4-5 in continuous rain. Eleven months later the handsome Milanese was killed in a testing accident at Modena. It was a prelude to a final tragedy which ended the Mille Miglia. The Marquis Alfonso de Portago, a Spanish nobleman who had achieved sporting success as a steeplechase jockey and in the Winter Olympics, was a member of the Ferrari team.

Twenty-five miles from the finish in Brescia, Portago's Ferrari burst a tyre. It went off the road killing 10 spectators.

Portago and his passenger Ed Nelson also died. The race, a sad victory, went to Italian veteran Piero Taruffi after Briton Peter Collins in another Ferrari was prevented from equalling Moss's triumph when his car failed almost in sight of the finish.

It was the end of the race. The Italian authorities refused to let it continue. Even without the terrible accident its future was probably curtailed. The event was causing unacceptable delays and traffic hold-ups in an increasingly urban and motorised Italy. It was run as a regularity trial for several years then abandoned.

In the 1990s it was revived, not as a race but as a regularity run over the 1954-57 course for historic cars of the type which competed in the original series. It has become the magnet for every classic and historic race driver and is regarded as the pinnacle of this class of competition. Drivers come from all over the world and the entry list is always over-subscribed. For those who take part, or even spectate, the magic of the remarkable, testing and unique Mille Miglia lives on.

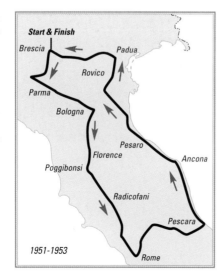

*Stirling Moss and Denis Jenkinson
are pictured during their
legendary drive to victory in 1955
with a Mercedes-Benz 300SLR.*

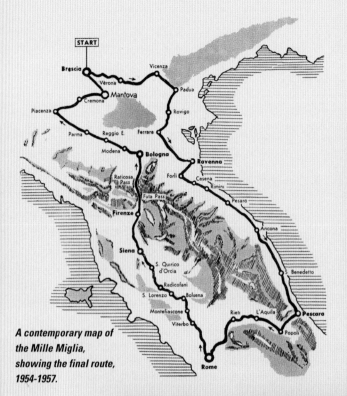

A contemporary map of
the Mille Miglia,
showing the final route,
1954-1957.

*The scrutineering of the
entries in Brescia forms a
colourful scene before the
1956 race.*

*An OSCA takes the flag
at the finish of the 1956
Mille Miglia.*

CHAPTER 12

Nürburgring

An all-Mercedes-Benz front row is appropriate at the opening race of the Nürburgring in June 1927.

KNOWN as 'The Ring' to countless enthusiasts world-wide, the Nürburgring was the most testing circuit ever used for an F1 World Championship race. Its only rival for this honour would be Pescara.

The Ring was devised in the 1920s as a racing circuit and test track for the German motor industry. The construction was also to provide work for many unemployed workers who were suffering in the economic woes of the Weimar Republic.

The initial idea is credited to Dr Creutz, a local councillor in the Eifel district west of the Rhine. He enlisted the support of Konrad Adenauer, the Oberbürgermeister of Cologne. Adenauer would later make history as the Chancellor of the post-war Federal German Republic and as a major architect of the post-war German economic revival. Adenauer persuaded the German government to fund the project with a contribution of 15 million marks.

The track was designed by the Eichler Architekturburo in Ravensburg. The concept was remarkable. A site was chosen south of the small town of Adenau in the Eifel mountains. In the centre of the site was the 12th century Schloss Nürburg which gave the circuit its name. Plans were drawn up for a 17.58-mile (28.28km) circuit split into two loops, the 14.17-mile (22.79km) Nordschleife and the 4.8-mile (7.72-km) Südschleife.

The concrete roadway had an average width of 26-30ft (8-9m). Both loops shared a magnificent pits and grandstand complex. The full circuit contained 172 corners, 88 left-hand and 84 right-hand, of an infinite variety. The track swooped up and down through the mountains. On the North Loop there was a final 1.8-mile (3.0km) undulating straight to the finish.

The foundation stone was laid by Dr Fuchs, President of the Rhineland, in September 1925. Two years later the vast project was finished. The first meeting, the Eifelrennen for motorcycles and sports cars, was held on 19 June 1927. The winner of the first race was Rudi Caracciola in a 7.1-litre S-type Mercedes. Caracciola and the Ring would soon become synonymous.

The Eifelrennen meeting was a curtain-raiser for the main show, the German Grand Prix. This was held on 17 July, again using both North and South Loops. It was an 18-lap sports-car race, pulling in 75,000 spectators. It was a clean sweep for the S-type Mercedes which took the first three places. The victorious driver was Otto Merz, who had played a small part in world history as the chauffeur of Archduke Franz Ferdinand when he was assassinated at Sarajevo on that fateful day in June 1914. The Ring had shown it was tough, especially on tyres.

The two-loop circuit was used again for the Grand Prix in 1928. On a sweltering day 41 sports cars took the start. Once again it was a Mercedes win, this time for Caracciola with his uprated Type SS. The Ring claimed its first victim when Czech driver Cenek Junek, sharing his Bugatti with his wife Elizabeth — perhaps the greatest woman racer of all time — was killed when he overturned.

In 1929 the first major foreign win came in the Grand Prix, still a sports-car race. It was dominated by a team of Bugattis which were more suited to the twists and turns than the heavy Mercedes. The winner was French ace Louis Chiron, who refreshed himself with champagne at a pit stop, then *certainement* drank a lot more after the race.

The economic depression of 1929 silenced the Ring for two years. The Grand Prix came back in 1931 when only the Nordschleife was used. The Südschleife fell into disuse until 1960. In heavy rain, Caracciola beat the pure racing cars with a stripped SSKL sports Mercedes.

In 1932 the Grand Prix was the final and decisive round in the European Championship, forerunner of the World

Championship. The season had been dominated by the Alfa Romeo team. Its three drivers, Nuvolari, Borzacchini and Caracciola—who had left Mercedes—all had a chance to become Champion. Alfa policy decided that a German driver should win his home race. Nuvolari, who suspected his pit crew were deliberately going slow at his pit stop, threatened them with a hammer and came second to become Champion!

When the Nazis came to power in 1933 they decreed that motor racing should be a demonstration of German virility. The Ring was confirmed as the national centre of the sport. It was festooned with swastika banners while storm troopers paraded amidst all the pomp of Nazidom.

Some races mark a turning point in motor racing history. The 1934 Eifelrennen was one of these. Both Mercedes-Benz and Auto Union raced their Grand Prix cars together for the first time. A Mercedes won and an Auto Union was second. For the following five years the rest would have little chance of success.

An embarrassing setback came in 1935, when Nuvolari, in one of the all-time legendary drives, beat the German teams in an outclassed and under-powered Alfa Romeo. Thereafter the top step of the German Grand Prix podium was shared between Mercedes-Benz and Auto Union drivers until war intervened in 1939.

The 1936 Eifelrennen were run in rain and mist. The new Auto Union ace, former motorcyclist Bernd Rosemeyer, amazed the racing world by driving through the fog to win at unabated speed. The centrepiece of the Eifelrennen was the race for Grand Prix cars, but there were supporting sports-car and voiturette races. The latter brought success to Maserati and the British newcomer ERA. Germany made few *voiturettes* so the class was abandoned after 1936. It was unacceptable to the Nazis to see foreign cars getting any glory. A slight dilution of German supremacy was evident in 1938 when Briton Dick Seaman, at the wheel of a Mercedes, won the Grand Prix, beating all the German aces.

After World War 2 Germany was not

A group of Mercedes SSKs and a Renault 45 leave the start at the 1929 German Grand Prix. German hopes are dashed when victory goes to Bugatti.

On the day that changed Grand Prix racing forever, Manfred von Brauchitsch takes the flag with his Mercedes-Benz W25 in the 1934 Eifelrennen.

A Mercedes-Benz W154 winds through the tortuous bends of the 'Ring' during the 1939 German Grand Prix.

The start of a 500cc Formula 3 race in 1950 sees a Cooper matched against DBs, Scampolos and Monopolettas.

re-admitted to the FIA until the end of 1949. Meanwhile the war-scarred Nürburgring was resurfaced and its buildings repaired. In 1950 the German Grand Prix was revived as a 2.0-litre Formula 2 race. It was won by rising star Alberto Ascari in a V12 Ferrari.

The full Grand Prix cars were back in 1951, effectively the last year of the 1½-litre/4½-litre formula. It was a bitter fight between the previously all-powerful Alfas and the Ferrari newcomers. Ascari's Ferrari won and Fangio's Alfa came second after losing all its gears but top. So awesome was this display that Mercedes-Benz put on ice the plans it had previously confirmed to build a new team of 1½-litre supercharged car.

The Eifelrennen disappeared from the calendar in the early 1950s, replaced by the 1,000km for sports cars which became a round in the World Sports Car Championship. For an earlier generation of Germans it seemed like old times again in 1954. Mercedes had returned to Grand Prix racing and its Juan Fangio swept to victory in the Grand Prix. After the Le Mans disaster there was no race in 1955, but Fangio did it again in 1956, this time in a Maserati leading home a mere five finishers.

Nineteen fifty-seven saw one of the truly great Grand Prix drives, when Fangio equalled and arguably surpassed

Walter Gotschke gives his dramatic impression of the bitter duel between Alfa Romeo and Ferrari in the 1951 German Grand Prix.

Nuvolari's feat in 1935. Against heavy odds, stopping to refuel his Maserati 250F, he came from behind to win against Hawthorn and Collins on Ferraris.

The 1,000km had become a major fixture in the calendar. Between 1957 and 1960 there were two hat tricks. Aston Martin won the race three times between 1957 and 1959, the last win contributing to their World Sports Car Championship. Stirling Moss won the race three times between 1958 and 1960, twice for Aston Martin and once for Maserati.

In 1960 the Grand Prix was held for 1.5-litre Formula 2 cars as a curtain-raiser to the 1961 Formula 1. After its 30-year slumber the Südschleife was patched up for the race. It was a wet day but the crowd was delighted by a German win. A Porsche came home in front, driven by Swede Jo Bonnier.

The character of Grand Prix racing was changing. Engines were now behind the drivers and British cars were triumphant. It was back to the Nordschleife in 1961. With his underpowered Lotus Stirling Moss out-drove the Ferrari team, clear pre-race favourites, to take the flag. It was reported that 270,000 watched him win.

In 1962 four cars duelled for the lead all the way, never more than four seconds apart in a downpour of rain. Graham Hill, who won in a BRM, said he considered stopping but then

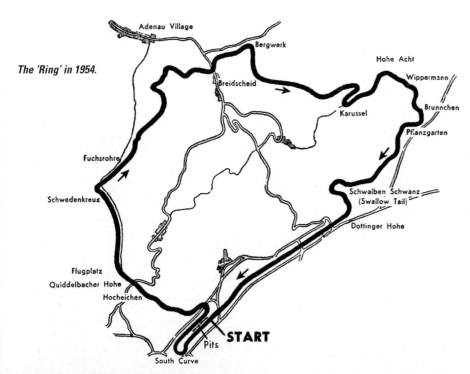

The 'Ring' in 1954.

Luigi Villoresi takes his Ferrari 375 F1 round the banked Karussell curve in the 1951 German Grand Prix. He finishes in fourth place.

The Ferrari 250TR of Tony Brooks and Jean Behra gets attention in the pits during the 1959 1,000 Kilometres. They finish third.

JUAN MANUEL FANGIO

Although over half a century has elapsed since he drove his last race, the name of Juan Manuel Fangio is still spoken with reverence whenever motor racing enthusiasts meet. But when his drive in the 1957 German Grand Prix is recalled, awe replaces reverence.

Fangio was no stranger to the Nürburgring. In 1951 he had brought an ailing Tipo 158 Alfa into second place, struggling through the closing laps with only top gear. He took another second in 1953. Then in 1954, to German delight, he secured a win for Mercedes-Benz. Another win on the Ring came in 1956, when he dominated the race in a Lancia-Ferrari, leading from flag to flag.

In 1957 Fangio had returned to Maserati, which to him was something of a favoured home team. Though their 250F was reaching the end of its life as a front-line Grand Prix car, chief engineer Giulio Alfieri had substantially updated it for 1957. Arriving at the Ring Fangio led the World Championship. He craved a win there, which would put the title out of reach of his youthful rivals.

At the age of 46 Fangio knew he would be challenged to win at the Ring. He accepted the strategy proposed by manager Nello Ugolini and chief mechanic Guerrino Bertocchi, which was to run as light as possible and refuel, with fresh tyres, at the mid-race point. This would be easier on the car on the bumpy, hilly Ring. Ferrari, in contrast, elected to run non-stop.

In practice Fangio set the pace by carving 26 seconds off his record pole time of the year before, giving an advantage of three seconds over his closest rival, Mike Hawthorn. In the race he took it easy at first to let his Pirelli tyres settle in. After three laps he swept by the Ferraris of Mike Hawthorn and Peter Collins to take the lead. They were relaxed, however, knowing that Fangio planned to stop.

Then the fireworks began. On five of the next nine laps Fangio broke the lap record, which had been 9.41. He carved huge chunks off this time, reducing it to 9.29 while striving to build up a lead for his planned stop. On lap 12 he came in with a 28-second lead. The team had planned a stop lasting 30 seconds. But the Maserati mechanics made a horrific bungle. The 250F was at the pit for almost a minute while fuel was added and the tyres changed.

When Fangio rejoined he was 45 seconds behind the Ferraris with ten laps to go. Again he used the first three laps to bed in his new tyres before opening the tap, then pulling back six or seven seconds a lap from the leading pair. The Ring's long lap meant that their pit had few chances to warn them. Juan turned lap 19 in an amazing 9:17, taking an unbelievable 23 seconds off the previous record. On his next lap Fangio soared past the Ferraris, whose helpless drivers watched him go on to win by 3.6 seconds. It was his last Grand Prix victory and one of the greatest of all time.

'Without any doubt,' Fangio reflected later, *'the Nürburgring was my favourite circuit. I loved it — all of it — and I think that day I conquered it. On another day it might have conquered me, who knows? But I believe that day I took myself and my car to the limit, and perhaps a little bit more.'*

The Lotus 33 (1) of Jim Clark shares the front row of the grid with the BRM P61s of Jackie Stewart and Graham Hill and the Ferrari 158 F1 of John Surtees at the 1965 German Grand Prix. Clark scores a resounding win by a margin of over two minutes.

thought, 'It's as bad for the others. I'll press on'.

Over the years the Ring had seen many fatalities, not only in races but also among enthusiasts who took their cars and motorcycles round the track. Many failed to appreciate its inherent dangers until it was too late. In the mid-1960s the number of fatalities among F1 drivers triggered a move to increase safety at circuits. There were hard looks at the Ring. Murmurs were heard that it was insufficiently safe, while diehards said it was the final true test of a great driver. Indisputably its great length made it impossible to assure quick rescue of an injured driver. In 1967 a chicane was built at the end of the main straight to slow cars entering the pit area.

Much of the campaign for the improvement of safety at circuits had come from Jackie Stewart. Although he disliked the Ring, calling it 'The Green Hell', he scored an impressive win in the 1968 Grand Prix. He raced through mist and rain to defeat the field in a Matra-Ford DFV with a winning margin of over four minutes. In a distinguished career it was perhaps his finest drive, made even more because he had broken his wrist in a Formula 2 accident earlier in the season and it had not fully healed.

The clamour for improved safety took the German Grand Prix away from the Ring in 1970. During that resting year some of the bumps and crests were eased off, Armco barriers were erected and the lines of some corners were eased. The Grand Prix came back in 1971. Perhaps comforted by the changes, Stewart won again. This time his margin was two and a half minutes. Despite his dislike he had an evident affinity with the Ring as he scored again in 1973. He led from start to finish followed all the way by Francois Cévert, his Tyrrell team-mate.

It all went sadly wrong in the 1976 Grand Prix. The suspension of World Champion Niki Lauda's Ferrari broke

The entries line up in front of the pits for the 'Le Mans' start of the 1966 1,000 Kilometre race.

Below left: *The Ford GT40 of Innes Ireland and Mike Salmon leaves the pits during the 1966 1,000kms. It retires after an accident on lap 13. No 67 is a Lotus Elan entered by a German team.*

The Alfa Romeo GTA of Manfred Hartung and Heinz Gilges leads a Shelby Cobra and a Lotus Elan during the 1966 1000kms.

Robert Kubica's BMW Sauber leads the Ferrari of Kimi Raikkonen in the 2008 German Grand Prix.

halfway round lap two. His car hit the barriers and burst into flames. By the time he was released Lauda was badly burned. His life was threatened for a time, though he recovered eventually, even going on to take another Championship.

This was the end for grand prix racing at the Ring. It was agreed that the circuit was too long for help to be available promptly if a driver crashed. There was another element. The TV rights of F1 were becoming hot property. TV companies preferred shorter circuits where a race could have continuous coverage. The German Grand Prix moved to Hockenheim.

The 1,000km continued, using the Nordschleife, but the circuit was modified and shortened to 12.9 miles (20.8km). The last 1,000km race was held on the Nordschleife in 1983. Thereafter no more serious racing graced the legendary track. In 1932 Nuvolari had lapped the circuit in 10 minutes 49.4 seconds. During practice for the 1976 Grand Prix, Lauda set the ultimate time with a lap in 6 minutes 58.6 seconds.

For the Eifel district the Nürburgring was a major economic factor. Its burghers realised that failure to take action could lead to disaster. In 1981 they initiated work on a new track. This was much in the modern idiom, straight lines broken by bends and chicanes for 2.8 miles (4.5km). It used the old pit straight, completely rebuilt, and ran over part of the site of the Südschleife. Although a mere shadow of the legendary old track which looms beside it, the new circuit brought the promise of new life.

It was first used for a World Championship round in 1984, hosting the Grand Prix of Europe. The race returned again in 1985 as the German Grand Prix, then there was a lull. The European event came back in 1995 and 1996. An expatriate Luxembourg Grand Prix was staged there in 1997 and 1998. The European race was run there regularly from 1999 to 2007. Using the 'European' title has enabled Germany to stage two World Championship rounds in a season. To German delight the new Ring became a happy hunting ground for Michael Schumacher. He won five Championship rounds there between 1995 and 2006. Another driver who showed an affinity was Fernando Alonso, who scored twice, in 2005 and 2007.

The Nürburgring still lives, albeit in name only. Now it is a clinical modern circuit hosting another Championship round. To enthusiasts with a feeling for history, however, the legends of the old Nordschleife will live forever. It was a circuit which was the ultimate test for man and machine. To win there was a truly great feat.

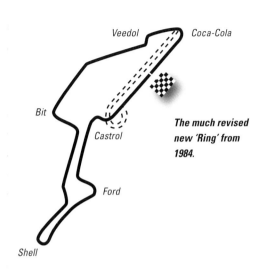

Veedol   Coca-Cola

Bit

Castrol

Ford

Shell

The much revised new 'Ring' from 1984.

Lewis Hamilton suffers a bad day in his McLaren-Mercedes MP4/24 in the 2009 German Grand Prix, finishing a lap behind the winner.

Below: The start of a race at a classic meeting on the new Nürburgring takes place on the start/finish straight, a part of the original legendary Nordschliefe.

CHAPTER 13

Monaco

At the start of the 1930 Grand Prix Borzacchini's Maserati T26B is surrounded by a horde of Bugatti T35s.

Top right: 'Williams', the Anglo-French ace who won the first Monaco Grand Prix in 1929, leads the field at Ste Devote with his T35C Bugatti on the first lap of the 1930 race. Tram lines are a feature of the early races.

EVEN in 1929 the concept of running a Grand Prix race through the narrow streets of a Mediterranean city was regarded as impractical and unrealistic. Eighty years on it is even more impractical and unrealistic. In spite of this — or because of it — the Monaco Grand Prix has become the most iconic and celebrated Grand Prix of all.

The circuit traces its origins to 1911. The Automobile Club de Monaco had organised the Monte Carlo Rally, which it continued into the 1920s. However the ACM was regarded as a mere provincial French Club by the all-powerful *Alliance Internationale des Automobile Clubs Reconnus* (AIACR), the FIA's predecessor as world governing body of motor sport. This offended the Principality, which wanted its club to have full international recognition. The AIACR stipulated that unless Monaco could organise an international event within its boundaries, no recognition would be forthcoming.

In February 1928 the Rally organiser Antony Noghès decided that a Grand Prix would be the answer. He had the full support of Prince Louis II, the ruler of the Principality. He turned to Louis Chiron, a native Monegasque, for advice on the circuit. Chiron, a rapidly rising Grand Prix star, was a member of the Bugatti team. Chiron and Noghès chose a 1.95-mile (3.13-km) circuit within the Principality which has remained virtually unchanged for 80 years. Though many races had run through towns and cities, this was the first to be held wholly in a built-up environment.

Twenty entries came in for the first race on 14 April 1929. The bizarre fuel-consumption Grand Prix formula was ignored. It was a straightforward no-holds-barred motor race. Among the sixteen starters a battle developed between Anglo-French racer William Grover-Williams, racing as 'Williams' with a green-painted Bugatti, and German ace Rudi Caracciola with a stripped sports SSK Mercedes. They swapped the lead several times during the 100 laps. The Mercedes was thirsty, making a stop of over four minutes to refuel and change tyres. This gave 'Williams' an unchallenged lead to the end. Critics had forecast that the field would be almost wiped out by early-lap crashes and that the race average would be snail-like. They were wrong. Nine cars finished with only one eliminated in a crash. The race average was 49.83mph (80.19km/h) with a fastest lap by 'Williams' of 52.69mph (84.79km/h). The critics were silenced and the race's future assured.

Despite his 1929 performance, Caracciola was barred from the 1930 race as his vast stripped-sports Mercedes was deemed to be 'unsuited to the course'. Puzzlingly, a second Mercedes driven by Count Arco was allowed to start. A notable non-starter was Enzo Ferrari who should have driven an Alfa Romeo. The race became a Bugatti battle with local lad Chiron

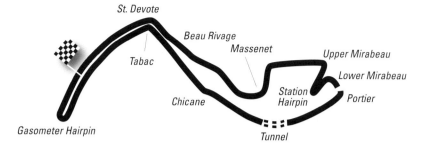

The Monaco circuit, 1929-72.

leading until his throttle stuck near the end, letting René Dreyfus, resident in nearby Nice, take the flag.

Louis Chiron had his revenge in 1931. A year later tram tracks and cobbles on some sections of the course were removed with some resurfacing. Now a major fixture on the calendar, the race pulled top-class fields. The Bugattis were vanquished by the Alfa Romeos and Nuvolari won from Caracciola who had changed his allegiance during years in which Mercedes wasn't racing as a factory.

In 1933 Caracciola, still in an Alfa, had a horrific crash in practice when he entered the Quai where the chicane now stands. His injuries nearly ended his career and left him out of action for over a year. During his convalescence Caracciola was nursed by Alice 'Baby' Hoffmann, Chiron's mistress, who eventually left Chiron to marry her patient.

The 1933 race set an important trend. It was the first major Grand Prix whose grid was decided by practice times. The fall of the flag heralded an historic legendary battle. Matched were bitter Italian rivals, Nuvolari and Achille Varzi. Nuvolari had an Alfa while Varzi was Bugatti-mounted. Their fight began after four laps with the lead changing constantly, often several times in a lap. The lap chart showed that Nuvolari led for 66 laps and Varzi for 34. By lap 90 Nuvolari had pulled out a four-second lead, but then Varzi reeled him in.

At the start of lap 98 of 100 the rivals crossed the line level. Varzi took the lead but lost it again as they rounded the Gasworks hairpin to start the last lap. Savagely over-revving his engine, he passed Nuvolari as they went up the hill from Ste Devote to the Casino. Nuvolari responded, trying to retake the lead in the tunnel, but his Alfa had enough. Its engine exploded in a cloud of smoke and oil spray. Varzi went on to take the flag. It contrasted with F1 racing in the modern era in that the cars never touched. Despite their bitter rivalry, each driver always gave room for the other to pass. The mortal risk in a collision was just too great.

The new era of Grand Prix racing began in 1934 when the German teams arrived. They gave Monaco a miss in 1934 but three Mercedes sat on the front row of the grid in 1935. It didn't go quite to plan as two dropped out, but Italian Luigi Fagioli, the swarthy 'Abruzzan Robber', led from start to finish to take the flag.

Luigi Fagioli takes the Gasometer Hairpin in his Mercedes-Benz W25 during the 1935 Grand Prix. He has an untroubled win, leading from flag to flag.

Rudi Caracciola wheels his Mercedes-Benz W125 into Casino Square during the 1937 Grand Prix. Though placing second, he sets a lap record which stands for 18 years.

Juan Manuel Fangio takes the flag in the 1950 Monaco Grand Prix with a Tipo 158 Alfa Romeo. This is his first Championship-round win.

It was wet for the first time in 1936. Oil put down by an Alfa at the chicane on lap one caught out two Mercedes, an Alfa and a Maserati in a multiple shunt on the next lap. The wet caused more crashes. Nuvolari coped with the conditions in his Alfa, but when his brakes faded he gave best to Caracciola who won in the surviving Mercedes from two Auto Unions. A supporting race for 1.5-litre *voiturettes* was run in the dry the previous day. The winner in an ERA was Siamese Prince Bira, starting two decades as a prominent player.

Next year, 1937, the race moved from April to high summer — mid-August. It was a Mercedes 1-2-3 and winner Manfred von Brauchitsch pushed the race average up to 63.27mph (101.81km/h). Such was the power and torque of the German cars that they raced in the Principality without shifting gear.

Racing engines were not heard again in the Monaco streets for eleven years. In a much-changed post-war world, Italian Giuseppe Farina took his Maserati to a two-lap win in 1948 over Chiron, now a greying veteran with a Talbot-Lago.

There was a fallow year in 1949, but 1950 saw the beginning of the World Championship. Monaco was the second round of the season. The wind carried sea spray onto the course at the Tabac. On the opening lap Fangio took the lead in his Alfa Romeo. Farina, leading the rest, spun his Alfa and the field piled into him. Ten cars were eliminated, though no one was hurt. Typically Fangio avoided the *carambolage* and carried on serenely to an unchallenged win. The supporting race for the new 500cc class went to a promising newcomer, Stirling Moss in a Cooper. Both he and Cooper would make their mark at Monaco in the years to come.

There was no race in 1951. Monaco became a sports-car race in 1952, marred by the first fatality. Veteran Fagioli crashed his Lancia exiting the Tunnel during practice, dying of his injuries three weeks later. Mercedes were back in 1955. An overwhelming win was expected. Uncharacteristically the three Mercedes team cars expired, so victory went to French champion Maurice Trintignant in a Ferrari.

Moss scored for Maserati in 1956 but was the catalyst for a pile-up in 1957. He misjudged the chicane when leading Ferrari rivals Hawthorn and Collins, who piled into the chaos. This left Fangio to take an untroubled win. The grid had been limited to 20 cars in 1955. In 1957 it was reduced to 16, eliminating the slowest in practice.

In 1956 Prince Rainier, Monaco's ruler, married American film legend Grace Kelly. The race winner in 1957, and in the following years until her death in 1982, had the additional reward of receiving the winner's plaudits from the comely princess.

The Lancia B20 of Salvatore Ammendola leads the Le Mans Replica Frazer Nash of David Clark into the chicane during the 2-litre supporting race at the 1952 Grand Prix. Clark finished in fourth place.

Reg Parnell stands beside his new DB3 before the 1952 Grand Prix. Driver Lance Macklin walks between the cars. Macklin's DB3 is behind. Parnell's car was wrecked when it was in a multi-car collision after he stopped with a broken engine and Macklin's engine broke too.

In 1952 the Grand Prix gives way to two sports-car races. The winner of the main event, Vittorio Marzotto, takes his Ferrari 225S through Tabac Corner.

Ascari takes his Lancia D50 into the chicane in the 1955 Grand Prix. Soon afterwards he crashed at this spot and he and the Lancia ended in the harbour. This was his last race; he was killed a few days later in a testing crash at Monza.

Gerino Gerini takes his Maserati 250F along the sea front during practice for the 1958 Grand Prix. He failed to qualify.

Cliff Allison in a Lotus 12 leads Francesco Godia-Sales with a Maserati 250F along the seafront during practice for the 1958 Grand Prix. Godia-Sales fails to qualify while Allison finishes seventh.

The early-morning sun shines on Wolfgang von Trips's Ferrari Dino 246 F1 during practice for the 1958 Grand Prix.

Italian Stanguellinis predominate at the start of the 1959 Formula Junior race. A year later British cars begin an unbroken rule of the class and the subsequent Formula 3. Victory in the Monaco F.Jr race was the aim of every aspiring young driver.

Monaco was the scene of a sea change in Grand Prix racing. Early in 1958 Moss had won the Argentine GP in a rear-engined Cooper. The racing world dismissed it as a fluke. At Monaco, however, Maurice Trintignant repeated the win with the same car entered by Rob Walker's plucky private team. Within a mere season the front-engined GP car joined the dinosaurs after a 60-year reign.

More history was made in 1960 when Moss scored with a Lotus, the first Championship win for the marque, leading home a mere four finishers. Scratching around at the back of the field was a rear-engined Ferrari. Like Canute, Enzo had tried to hold back the rear-engined tide for two seasons, but finally admitted defeat. Monaco saw the first Grand Prix Ferrari with the driver before the engine.

A year later the new-look Ferraris were in full flight. British manufacturers had been caught out by the formula change to 1½ litres. Moss came to Monaco with an underpowered Lotus. He led the much more potent Ferraris all the way to win what

many consider his greatest Grand Prix race. Monaco became a trend-setter. In 1961 the previous straw-bale barricades were replaced by Armco barriers; now on every circuit world-wide.

Traditionally the Monaco race was started from the waterfront after which the field immediately rounded the Gasworks Hairpin. Chaos intervened in 1962 when there was a multiple pileup. To avoid a repetition, in 1963 the start was moved round the corner to the following straight. The new layout saw the first win by Graham Hill who would become the uncrowned King of Monaco. He had a hat trick of wins followed by two more in 1969 and 1970.

Tragedy struck in 1967. Italian Lorenzo Bandini, leading the Ferrari team and running in a steady second place, clipped the barriers at the chicane with 20 laps to go. The car overturned and caught fire. Bandini died a few days later. His death was a further impetus for the campaign for safer racing.

Lorenzo Bandini had grown up in the tough school of Formula Junior. This training formula, introduced in 1958, caught on rapidly. From 1960 it became an annual Monaco curtain-raiser. The FJr race and the F3 race that replaced it from 1963 was the one every aspiring driver wanted to win.

GRAHAM HILL

Graham Hill gets the victor's spoils after his 1969 win. Team boss Colin Chapman spills the champagne.

Graham Hill came up the hard way. His was a true 'rags to riches' story, from racing mechanic to World Champion. After a spell with Lotus, where he began as a gearbox fitter, in 1960 Hill joined the BRM team which was beginning to come good. In 1962 a BRM took him to the World Championship.

Hill and Jim Clark were fierce yet friendly rivals. Hill just pipped Clark to the 1962 Championship. At Monaco in 1963 Hill staved off a charging Clark for 18 laps, then had a fight to defend second place from John Surtees's Ferrari. The Ferrari sickened, then on lap 79 Clark could find no gears. Hill sped by to win and receive the winner's garlands from Princess Grace.

A year later it was Hill versus Clark again. Clark led in his Lotus until a rear roll bar loosened. He stopped to remove it, then Hill passed American Dan Gurney into the lead. Clark set off after Hill, who was nursing an engine with low oil pressure, but it was the Lotus's Climax engine which broke with only four laps to go. Once again Hill cruised home to victory.

In 1965 Graham Hill must have expected a clear run in the Principality as Clark was away in the USA, driving in the Indianapolis 500. From the start it went well. He took an immediate lead but after 20 laps was balked by a slow car and took to an escape road to avoid a collision. He lost four places but plugged away steadily, picking off the two Ferraris and team-mate Jackie Stewart. After 65 laps he was back in front. Hill pressed on to get the royal garlands again, breaking the lap record on the way.

Hill left BRM to join Lotus in 1967, driving with Clark. When the team came to Monaco in 1968, Clark's tragic death was still being mourned. Hill had the new Lotus 49 with Cosworth-built Ford DFV engine. He dominated the race, taking the lead after four laps and pressing on to an unchallenged victory, mindful that Team Lotus needed a win for so many reasons. His World Championship that season was a tonic as well.

Drama preceded the 1969 Monaco race. At the previous Championship round, the Spanish GP, Hill and team-mate Jochen Rindt crashed when the wings on their Lotuses collapsed. The CSI (*Commission Sportif Internationale*) imposed a ban on wings as the cars arrived at Monaco. The ban forced Hill to race his 49-Ford in a virtually untested configuration. Undaunted, he moved up through the field. After 23 laps he led, going on to the flag and his fifth Monaco win.

Graham Hill's Monaco wins mirrored his career: gained by hard work, dogged determination and no little skill.

It was watched by every F1 team manager looking to spot future talent.

In 1968 the Monegasque race was shortened to 80 laps to comply with a new F1 rule which required a race to have a maximum distance of 200 miles (320km) or two hours' duration.

After 43 years the first major change came to the circuit in 1972. For safety the pits were moved to a new site between the chicane and the Tabac. A year later there were much bigger changes. With the harbour front widened, the track now ran along the edge of the new harbour wall before making two sharp turns round the swimming pool. It then ran on past the old Gasworks hairpin through a left-hand turn to a double corner, La Rascasse, then back to the pits straight. The pits were almost back in their old home, sited in a separate lane on the old sea-front section of the track. The tunnel was longer because the track was covered over by a gallery to house the new Loews Hotel.

The new circuit length was 2.03 miles (3.28km). The first lap record set by 'Williams' in 1929 had been 2:15. The ultimate lap record for the old circuit was set in 1971 by Jackie Stewart in 1.22.2. To comply with FIA rules, in 1973 the race distance was shortened to 78 laps. The first winner on the revised circuit was Jackie Stewart with a Tyrrell-Ford DFV, chased hard by the Lotus of Emerson Fittipaldi who set the new lap record at 1.28.1.

There had been problems with the number of entries. For many years, for safety reasons the organisers had permitted only 16 cars to start. The Formula One Constructors' Association had contracted with other race organisers to provide a Championship field of up to 25 cars, giving rise to suggestions that Monaco should be dropped from the Championship calendar. The circuit extension solved the problem, letting in a field of 25 runners.

With the rise and rise of sponsorship in Grand Prix racing the Monaco contest was no longer merely another race on the Championship calendar. It had become a major social event linked to the nearby Cannes Film Festival, a place for 'celebrities' to be seen, many basking on exotic yachts in the harbour.

Ferrari, mainstay of the Formula 1 field, had been through a poor patch. It came good for the red cars in 1975. Austrian Niki Lauda won, the first Ferrari success at Monaco for 20 years. He repeated the win a year later. The socialite crowd saw real drama in 1982. In the wet French ace Alain Prost led in a Renault until he spun off with 15 laps left and lost a wheel. After Ricardo Patrese's Brabham took the lead, he too spun off. On the last lap the Ferrari of Didier Pironi and the Alfa Romeo of Andrea de Cesaris, running one-two, both ran out of fuel so Patrese, who had restarted, took the flag.

Prost, 'The Professor', was not to be denied. He began a hat-trick of wins in 1984. His run of success was interrupted by his bitter rival Ayrton Senna who won in 1987. Prost was on top again the next year, then Senna had a straight run of five wins. For 10 years no other driver had a look-in. Then the new kid emerged on the block. In 1994 Michael Schumacher took the Monaco flag on the way to the first of his Championship titles.

Schumacher went on to win the race five times. In 2000, after a gap of 27 years, 'God Save the Queen' was heard again over the loudspeakers at the end of the race when Briton David Coulthard, who lived in Monaco, stood beside Prince Albert on the podium facing the pits. Coulthard was welcomed there

Among the wins which secure Denny Hulme the 1967 World Championship is this one in the 1967 Monaco Grand Prix with a Brabham-Repco BT20. He has more than a lap margin.

Above left: Jim Clark seems certain of victory in 1963, but the gearbox of his Lotus 25 breaks with only 20 laps to go.

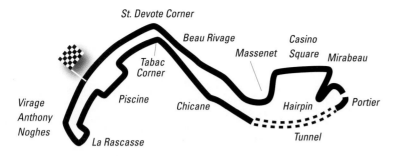

St. Devote Corner

Beau Rivage

Massenet

Casino Square

Mirabeau

Tabac Corner

Piscine

Chicane

Hairpin

Portier

Virage Anthony Noghes

La Rascasse

Tunnel

The Monaco circuit, 1973-2009.

Ronnie Peterson corners his Lotus-Cosworth 78 during the 1978 Grand Prix. He retires with a broken gearbox after 56 laps when running fourth.

again in 2002. For French enthusiasts Monaco is virtually a home circuit. Thus there was great joy when a Renault won in 2004, driven by Jarno Trulli.

Schumacher's last outing at Monaco in 2006 was marred by controversy. He was alleged to have spun deliberately at the Rascasse during qualifying practice. His Ferrari effectively blocked the track, preventing his rivals from improving their starting times and grid places, so crucial with a modern F1 car on Monaco's tight corners.

In 2007 a new talent emerged in his first F1 season to dazzle the Grand Prix world. Youthful Briton

Lewis Hamilton was right up at the front in his McLaren-Mercedes. He felt he should have won the Monaco race, suggesting that his McLaren team had 'adjusted' the pit stops to let his team-mate Fernando Alonso finish first. He had his revenge in 2008, taking the Monaco flag on his way to the Championship title. It was another British win in 2009 when Jenson Button, also a Monaco resident, cruised to victory in a Brawn-Mercedes.

Monaco is the jewel in the Grand Prix crown. The glamour of its setting and its ambience are unique. It rewards driving skills and concentration like no other circuit. One mistake and all is lost. It is the race every Formula 1 driver wants to win above all others. The critics who questioned the initiative of Antony Noghès have been confounded.

Above right: Gilles Villeneuve, seen at La Rascasse with his Ferrari 312T5 in the 1980 Grand Prix, finishes fifth after an unscheduled stop for tyres.

Alain Prost takes his Renault RE30 round La Rascasse during the 1981 Grand Prix. He pulls out with a broken engine.

Kazuki Nakajima with his Williams-Toyota FW31 seen taking the Loews Hairpin with the Casino in the background during the 2009 Grand Prix. Nakajima doesn't finish as he crashes at Mirabeau on the last lap.

Far left: **Michael Schumacher** *takes his Ferrari F300 within inches of the armco during the 1998 Grand Prix. It was a bad day as he finishes 10th, two laps down.*

Mark Webber retires his Williams FW28 after 48 laps with a broken exhaust in the 2006 Grand Prix.

CHAPTER 14

Bern (Bremgarten)

The Auto Unions and all bar one Mercedes-Benz are already out of the picture at the start of the 1935 Grand Prix, leaving behind the also-ran Alfa Romeos and Maseratis.

THE Bremgarten circuit in Bern led a short but sensational life. In its brief years of action it became established as a true classic. The Bremgarten is a park on the north-western outskirts of the city of Bern in Switzerland. Its 4.6-mile (7.2km) circuit was devised using a section of the main road from Bern to Lausanne, then branching off onto country roads in the park.

Though superficially simple, the Bern circuit was in fact demanding. The road was narrow, running through woods for much of the distance. Despite the proximity of the city it was rural in character, even running past a sawmill and alongside a quarry. The road surface was variable, some parts laid with stone cobbles. There were only two proper corners with the rest being fast curves. The pits and start line, at the nearest point to the city, were adjacent to a railway yard.

Bern was first used in 1931 for motorcycle races. It was the venue for the Grand Prix de Bern, whose winner was the British rider Stanley Woods riding a Norton. With its motorcycle races a success, the Automobile Club Suisse decided to promote the first Swiss Grand Prix in 1934. The idea of a Grand Prix captured the Swiss imagination. Bern was *en fête* with posters and publicity everywhere. The Grand Prix was the climax of a speed festival with motorcycle races, national races for Swiss drivers and a 1,500cc *voiturette* race.

The 750kg Grand Prix formula had been introduced at the start of the 1934 season. By August, when the Bern meeting was held, an established pattern had emerged. The German Mercedes and Auto Union teams were on top with the others chasing hard behind. Both German teams were there, accompanied by Bugatti and Maserati. The works Alfas, entered by Scuderia Ferrari, were absent. Having received several hidings from the Germans, they opted for a minor race in France that weekend.

The first Swiss Grand Prix was a good day for Auto Union. The rear-engined cars took a 1-2. It was an equally bad Mercedes day, two dropping out and the team's best finisher two laps behind the winner.

The 1934 race was marred by a fatal crash. The Ulsterman Hugh Hamilton, regarded by many as the

Caracciola passes the pits in his Mercedes-Benz W25 on his way to win the 1935 Swiss Grand Prix. This section of the circuit is paved.

best British driver at that time, died after his Maserati left the road on the last lap and hit a tree. Later investigations indicated he may have had a heart attack, causing the crash. Young Dick Seaman, driving an MG, won the curtain-raiser *Voiturette* Prix de Bern from 23 starters. Soon to be thought of as the top Briton, Seaman scored his first win of many in Switzerland.

In its natal car-racing year the Bern race was established as a leading event in the calendar, ranking with the French and German GPs. Its popularity owed much to its accessibility at the centre of Europe and its siting on neutral ground for the leading teams. In 1935 Mercedes had revenge. It was their turn to score a 1-2. In the wet Rudi Caracciola showed his mastery of the conditions, sweeping to win on the treacherous cobbles.

Once again the Bremgarten showed its darker side. German Hans Geier crashed his Mercedes in practice, leaving the road at 150mph (240 km/h) on the fast bend before the pits. The car was smashed to pieces. Geier was thrown clear to land under a car in the adjoining car park. Though grievously hurt, he eventually made a full recovery. In the Prix de Bern, now regarded as the top voiturette race of the season, Seaman won again, this time with an ERA.

Racing director Huber, the guiding force behind the Bremgarten races, was concerned about the speeds being achieved on the circuit's curves. He suggested to the drivers that chicanes should be installed in 1936, but received a strong 'thumbs down'. The drivers liked the challenges of the Bremgarten.

The pendulum of success swung back for Auto Union in 1936. It was a bad year for Mercedes whose cars were off the pace. Auto Union also had Bernd Rosemeyer, a true wonder driver who had burst into prominence. He led a 1-2-3 for the Porsche-designed cars from Zwickau. On his way to the flag, Rosemeyer set a lap record which would never be bettered; 2.34.5 (105.4mph/169.58 km/h).

In the preliminary Prix de Bern, Seaman was back again, this time with a revamped 1927 Delage. Too fast for the ERAs and Maseratis, it took Dick to a hat trick of Bremgarten wins. His drive was watched by Mercedes team manager Alfred

A contemporary Swiss map showing the Bern circuit.

Dominating the 1,500cc Voiturette class in 1936 with his rebuilt 1927 Delage, Richard Seaman is on the way to victory in the Prix de Berne. This is the second of his three consecutive wins in fourteen days.

Hans Stuck's Auto Union C-Type pulls out a slight lead over Rudi Caracciola's Mercedes-Benz W125 at the start of the 1937 Grand Prix, which Caracciola goes through to win.

Neubauer. Appreciating that he was seeing real talent, he took Seaman into the team for 1937.

For three seasons Alfa Romeo, racing with the Prancing Horse of the Scuderia Ferrari on its red cars, had tried to hold back the German hordes. The key to the sparse Alfa successes had been Tazio Nuvolari, who had scored both remarkable and improbable victories. Thus the racing world was stunned when Nuvolari appeared at the Bremgarten in 1937 to drive an Auto Union. It availed him little as it was a Mercedes 1-2-3, Caracciola again showing he was unbeatable in the wet.

Fighting for the lead on the opening lap, Bernd Rosemeyer slid off the road and only regained the course with a push from spectators. He pulled into his pit, explained that he had received outside help and declared that he was disqualified— a quixotic gesture unlikely to be seen in World Championship races of the 21st Century.

The *voiturette* world was split into two camps. North of the Alps ERA was dominant. South of the mountains Maserati held sway. Bern was the only circuit where the two teams met. In 1937 the ERAs ran away with the honours conclusively. It was a different story in 1938. As with the German teams,

RUDOLF 'RUDI' CARACCIOLA

Among students of motor racing history, there is a never-to-be settled question: who was the greatest driver of the golden era of the 1930s? For some there is no argument: it was Rudolf 'Rudi' Caracciola. Among his many remarkable drives they cite his performances in Berne's Bremgarten as conclusive proof.

Born in 1901, Caracciola began racing in 1922. Soon rising to eminence among his German contemporaries, by the beginning of the 1930s he had gained some remarkable wins in a Mercedes SSK, including the Mille Miglia and German Grand Prix.

A crash in practice at Monaco in 1933 left Rudi grievously injured, his recovery taking more than a year. When Mercedes made a triumphant return to Grand Prix racing in 1934, a not-fully-fit Caracciola was in the team. He came into his own in 1935 when he was headed in few races. He had already shown an uncanny ability to win races in the rain, earning the title 'Regenmeister' or 'Rain-master'.

It was dry when the flag fell to start the 1935 Swiss Grand Prix. Caracciola took his Mercedes into the lead. Then the rain chucked down. While other drivers slowed Caracciola pressed on, his pace virtually unaltered, lapping almost the whole field before taking the flag.

By 1938 Caracciola was being challenged by new drivers in the Mercedes-Benz team. Former mechanic Hermann Lang and British star Richard Seaman were striving for pre-eminence. Rudi enjoyed protection from team manager Alfred Neubauer, for whom Caracciola was a very special talent, a man whose many wins for the three-pointed star made him a man apart.

Dick Seaman had shown his talent by winning the German Grand Prix at the Nürburgring. When the teams came to Bern two weeks later, there was talk that he would repeat the victory. Expectations grew when he set the fastest practice lap.

When the cars lined up it was raining heavily. After taking the lead from Caracciola at the start, 10 laps later Seaman came up behind two slower cars. The Englishman eased, waiting for a suitable place to pass in the conditions. Caracciola saw his chance. He swept past Seaman and the two backmarkers in one imperious move, seemingly indifferent to the downpour. His performance was all the more amazing as he had lost his visor and was driving only with goggles. All Seaman could do was to follow Caracciola to the end of the race, some 26 seconds behind.

There was an ironic Bremgarten sequel. Caracciola was badly hurt when he crashed in practice for the 1946 Indianapolis 500, his first post-war race. He didn't compete again until 1952, taking the wheel of a Mercedes 300SL coupé when the German company returned to the sport. After placing fourth in the Mille Miglia he drove a 300SL in the sports-car race preceding the Swiss Grand Prix. When a rear brake locked he crashed head-on into a tree. Badly injured, Caracciola recovered but never raced again.

In 1959 Rudi Caracciola died of a liver infection at the age of 58, having spent his last years as an ambassador for Daimler-Benz. No one was better qualified.

The 1938 Grand Prix was run in heavy rain. Caracciola masters the conditions in his Mercedes-Benz W154 to go on to win.

Giuseppe Farina sweeps past the crowd in his Alfa Romeo Tipo 158 on his way to win the 1950 Grand Prix. With such poor crowd safety, accidents involving spectators were inevitable.

The tricky Bremgarten catches out even experienced racing drivers. Henri Louveau escapes unhurt when his Lago-Talbot leaves the road in the 1951 Grand Prix. The Lago-Talbot of Belgian band leader Johnny Claes passes.

the pendulum swung. Swiss Armand Hug brought his Maserati home in front of the British cars.

Despite his knowledge of the circuit, Seaman had been 'rested' by Mercedes in 1937. He was back in 1938. The Swiss Grand Prix was now being run to the new 3.0-litre blown 4.5-litre unblown formula which had commenced at the start of the season. On another wet day Seaman led until Caracciola, always at ease in the conditions, went past to take the win. Seaman came home in second place.

A depressed motor-racing circus arrived at Bern in 1939. Mercedes was still mourning the death of Seaman at Spa a few weeks earlier. On the wider stage war seemed inevitable. It was in reality only two weeks away. German dominance had taken its toll of the Grand Prix fields, which were dwindling as the opposition gave up.

To boost the field, the Swiss organisers invited the faster voiturettes to race against the full Grand Prix cars. Italy had abandoned Grand Prix racing in 1939 and embraced the voiturette class. Dominating the class — apart from a humiliating setback at the hands of Mercedes at Tripoli — was

the team of Tipo 158 Alfas. The Alfas came to Bern to race against Mercedes-Benz and Auto Union.

The 1939 race had separate heats for the voiturettes and Grand Prix cars with both classes meeting in a final. To German astonishment and Italian delight, Giuseppe Farina held his Alfa in second place for many laps until finally being overcome by German might. Caracciola had to give best to the new Mercedes star, Hermann Lang. With the race over, the British voiturette drivers made a dash for the Channel ports before war engulfed them.

Neutral Switzerland escaped World War 2 with minimal harm, allowing the Swiss Grand Prix to be revived in the Bremgarten in 1947. It was the first major race of the new Formula A, soon to be re-named Formula 1, for blown 1½-litre and unblown 4½-litre cars. The race drew all the big players including the all-conquering Alfa Romeo team. It was run in two heats and a final.

Crowd control was non-existent with spectators lining the edge of the road all round the circuit. On the slowing-down lap at the end of the first heat, a small boy ran across the track and

Two factory-entered 300SL Mercedes-Benzes share the front row of the grid with a Ferrari in the sports-car race at the 1952 Swiss Grand Prix. Karl Kling wins in his Mercedes.

was hit by the winning car, Varzi's Alfa. There was a delay while the police tried to push the crowd back. In the second heat Briton Leslie Johnson in a stripped sports Talbot-Lago hit two spectators who were standing on the road and killed both. Before the final the drivers were asked to back off and drive more sedately. There were fears that if the race were cancelled the crowd would riot. A sad race saw an Alfa 1-2-3.

More tragedy followed in 1948. During practice Achille Varzi went off the road in his Alfa, which overturned. Following was his great rival of the 1930s, Louis Chiron. Chiron stopped and was cradling Varzi in his arms when he died a few minutes later.

Worse was to come. The Italian motorcycle ace Omobono Tenni was killed during practice for the 500cc race. In the Grand Prix, with the inflated title of European Grand Prix, leading Swiss racer Christian Kautz was killed when his Maserati was involved in a collision with two other cars. It was the most grievous Grand Prix since the 1933 Monza debacle.

At the request of Varzi's widow the Alfa team continued to race and win, but withdrew from racing for the 1949 season. The 1949 Swiss race witnessed the first victory in a national Grand Prix for the emerging Ferrari team. New boy Alberto Ascari, son of a famous father, took the flag in front of team-mate Luigi Villoresi.

The Alfa Romeos were back in 1950 when the Swiss Grand Prix became a round in the newly instituted World Championship. The Championship was a battle between two Alfa team members, Nino Farina and Juan Fangio. At Bern Fangio's Alfa dropped out with a cracked valve seat, Farina taking the flag on his way to the title. The Prix de Bern was revived as a Formula 2 race. It was a Ferrari-Gordini battle among whose entries were two familiar names of an earlier decade, Hans Stuck and Hermann Lang.

The rain poured down again in 1951 for the Bremgarten race, the first round of the World Championship. By now the Ferraris were challenging the Alfas. In the wet Fangio won, gathering points for his first title. The Prix de Bern hadn't been repeated so the F2 cars ran with the big boys to make up a field of 21 cars.

The nature of GP racing changed in 1952 when, by mutual consent, Formula 1 was virtually abandoned. The World Championship was run for the 2.0-litre Formula 2 cars. This gave a real shot in the arm to the sport as it brought in much more varied fields.

The Bremgarten meeting saw more tragedy. In the motorcycle races in the morning before the Grand Prix two riders were killed, one the Italian sidecar champion Ercole Frigerio. The Prix de Bern became a supporting sports-car race.

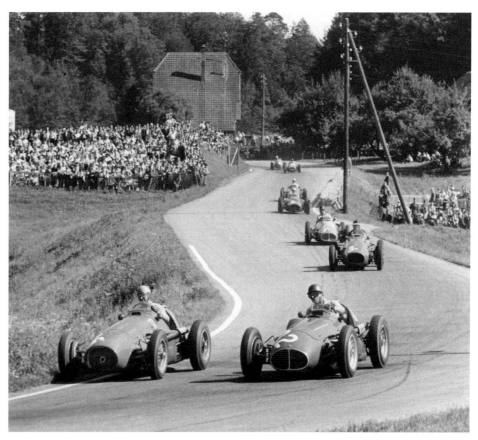

Ascari cuts his Ferrari 500 F2 inside the Maserati A6GCM of Fangio on the opening lap of the 1953 Grand Prix, while Hawthorn's Ferrari holds third. This becomes one of the five wins that secure Ascari the 1953 World Championship.

After the war Mercedes had stood quietly by, but a comeback came in 1952 with a team of 300SLs which ran at Bern.

Caracciola was in the Mercedes team, also making a return after serious injuries at Indianapolis in 1946. In the race he went off the road and hit a tree. Eventually he recovered but racing was now in the past for the great Rudi. The Ferrari Prancing Horse had become as omnipotent as the earlier Alfas so a Ferrari win in the Grand Prix was no surprise. The victorious driver was grey-haired Italian veteran Piero Taruffi.

During the 1930s the Bern meeting had been held in August. After the war it moved to May, but in 1953 it was back to August. The season had been dominated by Alberto Ascari and his Ferrari. A win on the Bremgarten circuit would clinch his second World title. He did not disappoint his fans. He led the race in the early laps, then stopped for a plug change. After that he zipped past his rivals to win comfortably and become Champion.

With the move to the 2½-litre formula a year later, Mercedes were back in the Grand Prix field. Team leader Fangio was unstoppable, romping away to take the Swiss Grand Prix. Over the years the Swiss national races had been a regular part of the meeting. After the war, one driver dominated these with almost monotonous successes. With his 4½-litre V12 Alfa

In an unusual perspective by Rodolfo Mailander, Stirling Moss takes his Maserati 250F through a downhill sweep during the 1954 Swiss Grand Prix behind the Ferrari of Froilan Gonzalez.

sports car Willy Daetwyler won the race every year from 1949 until 1954. An earlier national race winner had been Baron Emmanuel de Graffenried who became a regular and successful Grand Prix competitor for many years.

The Swiss Grand Prix was in the 1955 racing calendar. Then came the terrible Le Mans disaster. The Swiss government reacted more severely than other European nations by imposing an immediate ban on motor racing. Only rallies and hill climbs were permitted. The ban has remained ever since.

The testing and unforgiving Bremgarten circuit was never used again. With the emphasis on racing safety that came in subsequent years its long-term future would probably have been doubtful. It took too big a toll. Much of the circuit has now disappeared under road widening and improvements. Traces can still be found amid the trees of this remarkable and legendary track.

In 1982 an attempt was made to revive the Swiss Grand Prix with an expatriate race on the French Dijon-Prenois circuit. The experiment was not repeated.

Juan Manuel Fangio drifts his W196 Mercedes-Benz on his way to win the 1954 Swiss Grand Prix.

Fangio takes the corner before the pits in the 1954 Grand Prix, his Mercedes-Benz W196 followed by the Ferrari 625 F1 of Gonzales. Fangio wins with fellow Argentinean Gonzales second.

CHAPTER 15

Donington

T. K. Humber's Bugatti T37 leads two Frazer Nashes and an Aston Martin round the Hairpin at a club meeting in October 1934.

*Right: **Richard Shuttleworth, taking the flag at the first Donington Grand Prix in 1935 with his Alfa Romeo Tipo B. During the 30s Richard built up a sizeable collection of old cars, and somewhat later, aeroplanes, restoring them to working order. These now form the nucleus of the Shuttleworth Collection at Old Warden Aerodrome in Bedfordshire, which was also constructed by him. He joined the RAF in 1939 and was killed in a flying accident in 1940 in a Fairey Battle whilst on a night cross-country training excercise.***

I N Britain, from the very beginnings of motoring, racing on public roads was forbidden. While across the English Channel races were run on public roads on a myriad of circuits, the British enthusiast had only hill climbs on private roads or racing on the concrete bankings of Brooklands. Apart from occasional events in the Isle of Man and Northern Ireland, there was no road racing in Britain.

In the Midlands, between Leicester and Derby, was a country estate, Donington Park. Formerly owned by the Earls of Huntingdon, during World War 1 it was a prison camp for German officers. Donington Park was bought by John Gillies Shields who turned Donington Hall, the impressive house in the centre of the park, into a hotel.

In 1931 Shields was approached by Fred Craner, the secretary of the Derby & District Motor Club. Craner, who had been a motorcycle racer in the 1920s, suggested that roads and tracks in the park could be used for motorcycle racing. The first such meeting, held on Whit Monday 1931, was followed by others.

With increasing ambition, Craner suggested that the roads and tracks should be widened and surfaced with tarmac to make a circuit suitable for cars. Shields agreed, so the work went ahead. The original circuit cost £12,000, approximately half a million pounds in the values of the 21st century.

A 2.19-mile (3.52km) circuit was created. It ran across meadows and through woods, passing through a farmyard and under an ornamental stone bridge. The Derby & District Motor Club organised the first meeting on 25 March 1933. It was a fine spring day, drawing a gratifyingly large crowd for a programme of short races limited to cars of up to 1½ litres.

The fields were made up of stripped sports cars, mainly driven by amateur or 'club' drivers, though two well-known drivers, Eddie Hall and Freddie Dixon, took part. Hall had the distinction of winning the first race with an MG, obeying the rule that passengers had to be carried. Although some of the fields were thin — one race had only two starters — racing was close.

A second meeting was held in May 1933, again with close racing though some of the driving was more hair-raising than skilful. Nine thousand spectators had watched the racing, so

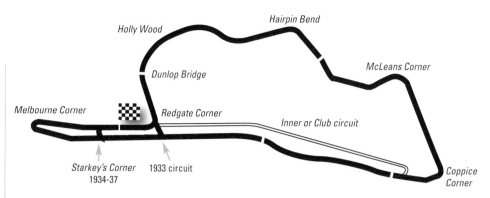

the venture promised financial success. At the third meeting in August, larger cars were permitted to race. Alas, a Bugatti left the road during practice, hitting a tree. The passenger died on the way to hospital. Thereafter the passenger requirement was abandoned.

The final meeting of the first season was held in October, when it rained. With Donington being taken seriously by the racing community, many leading British drivers entered. The major race of the day, the Donington Park Trophy, was over 20 laps and won by Earl Howe, in a Bugatti.

During the winter of 1933 the road was widened and some bends were eased. The circuit was extended with a loop which gave a lap distance of 2.55 miles (4.1km). After four minor meetings in 1934, drawing some major drivers, the final meeting in October was much more serious. There were two big races. The Donington Park Trophy for the bigger cars drew the Anglo-American heir Whitney Straight. The 22-year-old Straight had been running a professional team of Maseratis in the continental Grand Prix circus during the 1934 season. He ran away with the 20-lap Trophy race.

The last race in October was the 40-lap Nuffield Trophy for 1½-litre cars, presented by tycoon Lord Nuffield. A disparaging contemporary comment described the Trophy's design as 'a single-seater racing car ploughing through a sea of plasticine'. The winner of the Trophy was an ERA, the new British contender, given its first major win by its progenitor Raymond Mays.

Donington grew up in 1935. In addition to its minor meetings, the Nuffield Trophy in July was extended to 60 laps and saw another ERA win, this time for South African Pat Fairfield. The big one came in October, at the end of the season: the Donington Grand Prix, a proper 750kg formula race, the first to be held in Britain. A 306-mile (492km) race over 120 laps, it drew the fastest cars in England and even a works Maserati from Italy, driven by Giuseppe 'Nino' Farina.

Fred Craner's entreaties to the German Auto Union and Mercedes-Benz teams were rebuffed. Farina led the Grand Prix on a wet day until his V8 Maserati broke. At the end it was Briton Dick Shuttleworth who won in an Alfa Romeo. Shuttleworth would soon abandon cars for aircraft and found the remarkable Shuttleworth Collection of historic aircraft before being killed early in World War 2.

An extra boost came at the beginning of 1936. The British Racing Drivers' Club moved one of its major races, the British Empire Trophy, from Brooklands. It was won by rising star Dick Seaman in the Maserati with which Whitney Straight had won the Donington Trophy two years before. The Nuffield Trophy in July was another ERA win.

August 1936 brought yet more indications that Donington was becoming the major British circuit. In 1921 the Junior Car Club had instituted the 200 Mile race at Brooklands. This rapidly became a classic, but was abandoned after 1928. It was now revived and staged at Donington. Dick Seaman had been dominating the *voiturette* class with his revamped 1927 Delage. He arrived at Donington for the '200' having won two continental races in the previous 14 days. Untouched after its previous triumphs, apart from a plug change, Seaman's Delage walked away with the '200'.

The Donington Grand Prix was now the major event capping the British season. Often challenging the German teams in 1935, 8C 3.8-litre Alfa Romeo was still the fastest of the rest. Swiss driver Hans Ruesch brought his 8C to Donington and asked Seaman to share the driving. The pair walked away

Donington circuit from 1933 to 1939 – showing the 1937-39 extension called Melbourne Corner.

Kenneth Evans's Alfa Romeo Monza leads Derrick Taylor's Bugatti T51 through Holly Wood during the 1936 Donington Grand Prix. Before World War 2 Donington was heavily wooded.

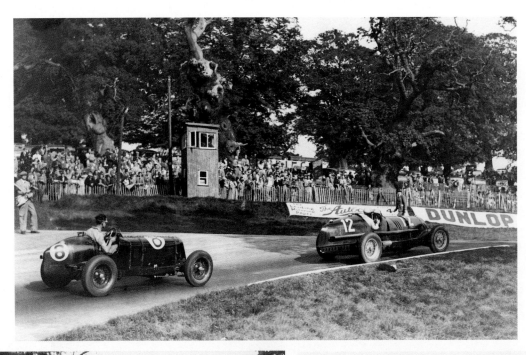

Hans Ruesch (Alfa Romeo 8C35) takes the Hairpin ahead of Peter Walker (ERA) in the 1936 Grand Prix. Ruesch wins, sharing the drive with Seaman, while Walker, sharing with Whitehead, places third.

Siamese Prince Bira in a Maserati 8CM leads Peter Walker's ERA through the bridge at the entrance to Coppice Wood in the 1937 British Empire Trophy. The Maserati retires with a broken gearbox and the ERA is third.

In the early laps of the 1937 Grand Prix, Seaman's Mercedes-Benz W125 leads the Auto Union C-types of Rosemeyer and Müller up the hill from the Melbourne extension which was built for the Grand Prix.

with 1936's 120-lap race by a three minute margin at the flag.

A short club circuit was introduced for the 1937 season. This was popular, with several clubs organising meetings. The British Empire and Nuffield Trophies were regular fixtures that saw wins for the works ERA team. In July the Derby club organised a 12-hour sports-car race. The first long-distance sports-car event to be held in England for five years, it was dominated by a Delahaye driven by Siamese Prince Bira. Two cars collided and the race had to be stopped briefly while the drivers were removed. Unfortunately one died later from his injuries.

After the 12-hour race Donington received an even bigger accolade. The RAC Tourist Trophy was still regarded by many as the premier British event. A sports-car race, this now came to Donington. For the TT early in September the circuit was lengthened further with an extension to the previous added-on loop. The lap distance was now 3.12 miles (5.23km). The Talbot-Lago and Gordini-Simca teams came from France and the BMWs arrived from Germany. The Talbots scored a 1-2 in front of 30,000 spectators. French driver René Le Bègue, who finished second, described the track as 'very difficult, but very interesting'.

In October 1937 Fred Craner finally achieved the prize he had been seeking since 1935. He secured entries from Mercedes-Benz and Auto Union for the Donington Grand Prix. Although it didn't have the title, it was in effect the British Grand Prix with all the major teams racing. Donington was now indisputably the top circuit in Britain.

The race lived up to all expectations. Between 40,000 and 50,000 turned up to watch, awed by the sheer power, speed and noise of the German cars. Much in the Formula 1 idiom of the 21st Century, the race was decided by refuelling strategies and tyre failures. At the end Bernd Rosemeyer's Auto Union took the flag ahead of the Mercedes of von Brauchitsch and Caracciola. The British entries were totally outclassed.

As at Brooklands, bookmakers on the course accepted bets. They didn't foresee the performance of the German teams and gave very good odds, taken enthusiastically by the German mechanics. When the outcome was certain the bookies disappeared! Craner and the Derby Club had to pay out their winnings to the German punters!

The 1938 season saw the Nuffield and British Empire Trophy races again as well as a string of club events. As in 1937, the big meetings came at the end of the season. The Tourist Trophy was run on 3 September. A good foreign entry found BMW, Bugatti, Delage, Lancia, Talbot-Lago and Simca-Gordini arriving to compete. Once again, it was a French victory. The winner was a Delage driven by Louis Gerard who made a prosperous living as an amusement-arcade operator in Paris.

The Donington Grand Prix was scheduled for 1 October. Both German teams entered and arrived at the circuit a week before the race. Meanwhile international tensions over the fate of Czechoslovakia had escalated. War between Britain and Germany seemed imminent. In desperate haste the German teams packed up and rushed for the Harwich ferry en route to the Fatherland. The Munich agreement over the Sudetenland

The Mercedes-Benz W125 of Manfred von Brauchitsch leaps as it crests the rise from the Melbourne extension in the 1937 Grand Prix.

Continued on page 132

Bernd Rosemeyer's Auto Union C-type makes full use of the verge on the way to winning the 1937 Grand Prix.

The RAC's sports-car Tourist Trophy is run at Donington in 1937 and 1938. The factory-entered BMW 328s of Prince Bira and Richard Seaman take Redgate Corner in 1938.

130

Nuvolari's D-type Auto Union out-sprints the W154 Mercedes-Benz of Hermann Lang at the start of the 1938 Grand Prix.

Hermann-Paul Müller's Auto Union D-type and Richard Seaman's Mercedes-Benz W154 race up the hill from the Melbourne extension in the 1938 Grand Prix. Percy Maclure's Riley is abandoned on the grass.

Tazio Nuvolari leads the opening laps of the 1938 Grand Prix with his D-type Auto Union . He takes the Hairpin ahead of his team mate Muller and a string of Mercedes-Benz W154s.

131

TAZIO NUVOLARI

THOSE who say Rudi Caracciola was the greatest driver of the 1930s face an equally partisan lobby for Italian Tazio Nuvolari. In 1938 Nuvolari was 42 years old. Fiercely patriotic, he had raced Alfa Romeos and Maseratis in Grands Prix long after these had become lost causes against the might of the German teams. In the spring of 1938 he announced that he was retiring from racing. There was no point in driving Alfas any more.

Three months passed. Then the racing world was amazed when Nuvolari appeared at the wheel of an Auto Union in the German Grand Prix. After the death of its great star Bernd Rosemeyer, Auto Union had been playing second fiddle to Mercedes in 1938, but Nuvolari revitalised the team. It took him two races to become accustomed to the revolutionary rear-engined machine. Then he won the Italian Grand Prix at Monza.

At the end of 1938 the top teams came to England for the Donington Grand Prix. In front of 60,000 spectators Nuvolari blasted to the front when

Nuvolari is acclaimed after winning the 1938 Grand Prix.

the flag fell. He led for 20 laps, seemingly running away with the race. Then his engine lost its note and he pulled into the pits for a plug change. Back in the race, he was running fourth when a backmarking British Alta burst its engine, putting down a swathe of oil. When Nuvolari encountered this he controlled his Auto Union with a few deft flicks of the wrist and sped on his way. Behind him cars flew everywhere.

After Nuvolari stopped again for fuel he was third, 70 seconds behind the leader. The crowd watched amazed. In ten laps he pulled back 35 seconds to move up to second. Each lap saw a new record. With 13 laps to go he caught the leading Mercedes-Benz of Hermann Lang. On the main Starkey Straight the Auto Union swept by the Mercedes into the lead. Even now Nuvolari didn't ease up. More lap records followed. At the finish after 80 laps he had a lead of 1 minute and 38 seconds.

With this astonishing tour de force of 1938 Tazio Nuvolari had made the best drivers in Europe look like beginners. It was almost his swan song. After one more major race victory at Belgrade in 1939, World War 2 intervened. When motor sports resumed in 1946, Nuvolari was a sick man. He raced and still astonished with some of his performances, but the great days of his career were over. Ill health took its toll and he died in 1953. He was 61.

defused the tensions. Fred Craner set a new date of 22 October and the German teams re-turned. On race day 60,000 spectators were the biggest crowd ever to attend a British motor race.

The race had royal patronage. The Duke of Kent, brother of King George VI, dropped the flag to start the race. Tazio Nuvolari, who had ultimately abandoned the lost Alfa cause and joined Auto Union, led from the start then lost nearly a minute with plug changes. Meanwhile one of the British backmarkers put down oil which took off several of the German cars. Nuvolari drove like a demon, clawed past the Mercedes opposition and went on to win.

Acclaimed by the crowd, he won £250 for first place and an extra £100 for fastest lap. This was about £15,000 by 21st-Century standards.

The British Empire and Nuffield Trophies were held in 1939, but the Tourist Trophy and Grand Prix scheduled for September were overtaken by the outbreak of World War 2. The last meeting was a club event on 12 August. Sadly this was marred by a fatal accident half-way through the meeting so the rest of the day's programme was curtailed.

When the war began, Donington was requisitioned by the War Office. Within a short time the circuit and park became the largest military vehicle park in Britain. When the war ended in 1945 hopes were high that the vehicles would be removed so the circuit could be used for racing again. With no racing circuits available in Britain, the need was desperate.

Despite endless entreaties, both the War Office and the vehicles remained unmoved. In the late 1940s Silverstone and Goodwood opened for business, as did other disused airfields that were suitable for racing. With the need for Donington no longer pressing, it gradually dropped from the consciousness of British enthusiasts.

After the last army lorry went in the mid-1950s talk began of a revived circuit but nothing came of it. In 1971 Donington was bought by Tom Wheatcroft, a local businessman. Wheatcroft, who had watched the pre-war grands prix at the circuit, was a great racing enthusiast who amassed an unrivalled collection of Grand Prix cars of earlier eras.

Tom Wheatcroft's first step was to move his car collection to a new purpose-built museum in the park to form the Donington Grand Prix Exhibition. A building contractor, Wheatcroft moved in the bulldozers. The circuit was completely rebuilt with a length of 2.5 miles (4.2 km).

Little of the former circuit remained. The line of the track was followed in some places and the names of the old corners were retained. The woods on the infield were removed to give spectators a view of most of the circuit. A new pit and paddock complex was sited across the line of the old main straight. Those who had known Donington before World War 2 found little they could remember. The result was a circuit in the modern idiom with all the features now expected in the motor racing world.

The first race meeting was held in 1977, beginning several seasons of club events. In 1985 an extension to the track enabled the Moto Grand Prix, the premier British motorcycle race, to be held at Donington. It has been an annual event at the circuit since 1987. A round of the British Touring Car Championship became a regular fixture.

In 1993 Wheatcroft and Donington achieved a major breakthrough. The track hosted the European Grand Prix, a round in the World Championship. It was famed for showcasing the astonishing talents of Brazilian Ayrton Senna. In heavy rain he started fourth on the grid. On the first lap he drove round his arch-rivals Prost, Damon Hill and Michael Schumacher to take an unchallenged lead. Witnesses praised it as one of the all-time great drives. Against expectations the Formula 1 circus did not return, though a four-hour sports-car and GT race was on the calendar for several seasons.

In 2008 Bernie Ecclestone, the boss of Formula 1, announced that an agreement had been signed that would give Donington the right to host the British Grand Prix for 17 years starting in 2010. A major circuit revamp was planned with a new infield loop extending the lap distance to 2.9 miles (4.7km). This was exciting news for a track well situated north of the British Midlands and with the pedigree of having hosted the great pre-war teams.

Unfortunately legal disputes, political infighting and lack of finance stalled the efforts of Donington's lessees to complete the necessary changes. At the end of 2009 the lessee company went into administration, and Donington lost the contract for the British Grand Prix. Whatever the future holds for Donington, it has a unique place in British motor racing history. It was the first road circuit in England and the venue where true Grand Prix racing came to Britain for the first time.

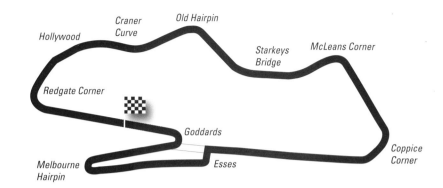

Donington Circuit, 1985-2009.

Damon Hill takes second place in the 1993 European Grand Prix with his Williams-Renault FW15C.

From its post-war reopening by Tom Wheatcroft until the end of the 2009 season, Donington was a popular venue for club events. This is the start of a vintage race in the 1990s.

CHAPTER 16

Hockenheim

*Above and right: **The Porsche 804 Grand Prix car is tested at Hockenheim by mechanic/driver Mimler early in 1962. It wins two races that year, one of them a Championship Grand Prix.***

THE town of Hockenheim is about 8 miles (13km) southwest of Heidelberg in the Rhine valley. In 1932 its burghers decided to put it more firmly on the modern map by building a racing circuit. A site was chosen in the forests east of the town. A 4.8-mile (7.7km) course was built which started on the outskirts and ran along a curve for almost two miles. It rounded a long gentle corner before returning to the town with a similar long curve. At the edge of town a U-bend took the course back to the start line.

The course was used for motorcycle racing, but racing cars came too. Mercedes-Benz and Auto Union found it a more practicable course for testing than the Nürburgring, so the silver cars of both teams thundered through the forests. In 1938 the track was renamed Kurpfelzring, a name it kept until 1947. The first car meeting, a minor club event for sports cars, was held in October 1938. The honour of being the first winner went to Ralph Roese with a Type 315 BMW.

The testing continued. In April of 1939 Mercedes-Benz, in great secrecy, was testing its 1.5-litre W165, built to shatter Italian class supremacy at Tripoli. During the testing the figure of Wilhelm Sebastian, Auto Union's development engineer, emerged from the shrubbery with a stop watch. Alfred Neubauer, the Mercedes team manager, shouted: 'Have you lost something?' 'A whole race, the Tripoli Grand Prix, I'm afraid,' replied Sebastian.

Economic problems and the logistical restraints of the occupying powers made the resumption of motor racing difficult in post-war Germany. When a meeting was finally staged at Hockenheim in May 1947, however, 200,000 spectators — starved of motor racing — came to watch. They saw pre-war Auto Union ace Hans Stuck win in an Italian Cisitalia. Other names that would soon loom large in German racing appeared. Karl Kling scored with a 1940 Mille Miglia BMW and Alex von Falkenhausen, later to be a guiding force with BMW, was also a winner.

The meetings, the Mai-Pokalrennen or May Trophy Races, continued in 1947 and 1948 with wins for the new BMW-based marques, Veritas and AFM. Racing moved up a rung in 1949 with an event for the new 2.0-litre Formula 2, though it only drew German entries. After that car racing was only sporadic for several years.

In 1954 Wilhelm Herz was appointed circuit manager. Herz, who had raced successfully for the NSU and DKW motorcycle

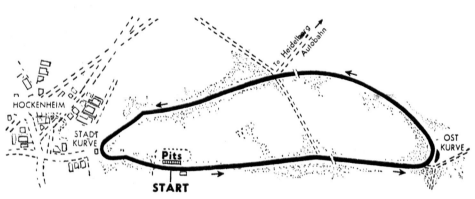

The Hockenheim circuit in 1954, fundamentally as it appeared from 1933 to 1965.

teams in the 1930s, was ambitious. He secured Hockenheim as one of the venues for the German Motorcycle Grand Prix. Herz promoted the Rhein-Pokalrennen, a round in the German sports-car championship in 1955, but it was an isolated event. It remained a fast circuit with a 1.5-litre Porsche 550 lapping at 111mph (179km/h) in 1955.

When Mercedes returned to the Grand Prix circuits in 1954, much of the early testing of the all-conquering W196 was done on the circuit. When the sports-car 300SLR appeared in 1955 it too had its first runs at Hockenheim. At the end of the 1954 season Mercedes were contemplating hiring the young Briton, Stirling Moss, as team driver. Given a trial, Moss secured his place by lapping a damp, leaf-strewn Hockenheim faster than team driver Karl Kling had done in the dry,.

In 1966 the A6 Autobahn was built — right across the section of the circuit that extended into the outskirts of the town. Outside the Autobahn a new section was built, linking the two fast curves. It was flanked by impressive grandstands and pits that became known as the Stadium. The circuit was shortened to 4.2 miles (6.8km). Another link road was built just beyond the Stadium to make an additional short circuit of 1.6 miles (2.6km).

Car racing was welcomed back to the shortened and improved circuit. A 1.6-litre Formula 2 race was held in 1967. Although a minor race, it had a major result. The winning Brabham, driven by Briton Robin Widdows, lapped at 125.76mph (202.34km/h). Immediately Hockenheim was up at the front as one of the fastest circuits.

A year later Hockenheim achieved international prominence for the saddest of reasons. At the beginning of April the Deutschland Trophy for F2 cars was held. Running in the first heat with a Lotus was two-time World Champion Jim Clark. For reasons that have never been fully explained, but that may have involved a tyre deflation, Clark went off the road at the end of the first long curve. With no safety barriers, his car hit the trees and he was killed instantly. The death of Clark, one of the most talented drivers of all time, shocked and saddened the motor-racing world.

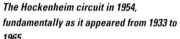

Clark's death was another incentive in the drive for greater motor-racing safety. At Hockenheim chicanes were built to reduce the cars' speed and safety barriers were erected. Racing went on, the nature of the circuit making for close slip-streaming battles. In 1969 the Formula 2 race was won by a margin of 0.3sec. It was tough on engines, with 60% of the lap run at full throttle.

In 1970 Hockenheim jumped unexpectedly to the top of the Grand Prix tree. Formula 1 drivers had been unhappy about the safety of the Nürburgring. Improvements had been started, but drivers were still unhappy and threatened to boycott the mighty Ring. At short notice the German Grand Prix was moved to Hockenheim. Its ultra-fast curves through the forest replaced the endless swoops and undulations of the Eifel mountains.

The move satisfied the crowd, who watched a wheel-to-wheel battle between the Ferrari of Jacky Ickx and the Lotus of German-born Austrian Jochen Rindt. Rindt won by the narrow margin of 0.7sec. It was a bittersweet victory. The win gave Rindt the points to hold a commanding lead in the World Championship, but his was a posthumous title. He was killed

In the second heat of the 1967 Formula 2 Deutschland Trophy, Pedro Rodriguez (Protos) and Chris Irwin (Lola 100) battle for the lead. They collide, spin off and fail to finish.

The Matra MS7s of Jean-Pierre Beltoise and Henri Pescarolo lead Piers Courage's Brabham BT23C in the second heat of the 1968 F2 Deutschland Trophy. It is a tragic day as Jim Clark is killed in the first heat.

Ostkurve

Sachskurve

The Hockenheim circuit 1966-1969.

At the start of the 1981 Grand Prix, Jacques Lafitte's Ligier JS17 leads the Ferrari 126CK of Gilles Vileneuve. They are followed by the McLaren MP4s of John Watson and Andrea de Cesaris. Lafitte finishes third.

during practice for the Italian Grand Prix five weeks later.

The Nürburgring was acceptable to the drivers in 1971 so the German Grand Prix returned there. Hockenheim was still a major F2 venue, running two races every season, the Deutschland Trophy and the Rhein-Pokalrennen or Rhein-Cup Race. In that era Formula 2 was popular, giving a chance for rising hopefuls to match their talents against the top F1 aces who were regular participants. It drew big fields; in 1971 there were 53 entries.

The near-fatal accident to Niki Lauda during the German Grand Prix at the Nürburgring saw the end of serious racing on the legendary Nordschleife. The German Grand Prix was back at Hockenheim in 1977. There was slight irony in that Lauda, whose fiery accident had cast a pall over the Ring, was the winner in a Ferrari on his way to the world title.

Hockenheim now became the established home of the Grand Prix. The lines of the chicanes were changed but otherwise it remained much the same. At the end of the 1978 race Jacques Lafitte, who came third, as a true son of France drank his champagne on the rostrum rather than spraying it, as had become the flamboyant custom.

This was the age of the controversial 'skirts' in Formula 1 and the high downforce they helped generate. In the week before the 1980 Grand Prix, Patrick Depailler, one of the new generation of French drivers, came to Hockenheim to test his Alfa Romeo. He went off on the fast East Curve, possibly because a skirt broke, and was killed when his car hit the

barriers. To slow the cars and prevent such an accident again, a chicane was built in the middle of the curve for the 1981 Grand Prix.

The 1980s witnessed the beginnings of the turbo era for which Hockenheim with its fast straights was ideal. In 1981 the Renaults were tipped to win, but Alain Prost had a faulty rev limiter which kept him in second place behind Nelson Piquet's Brabham. The circuit was not over-popular with the teams. It was regarded as an engine breaker. A team manager described it as two Autobahns linked by a curve.

The 1982 season was a black one for the Ferrari team. The popular and quick Gilles Villeneuve had been killed in a practice accident in Belgium. Ill fortune continued at Hockenheim, where Frenchman Didier Pironi's Ferrari collided with Prost's Renault in practice. Pironi recovered from his severe injuries but never raced cars again. He had set fastest lap, so his place on the front of the grid was left empty. To general satisfaction Patrick Tambay, recruited into the Ferrari team to fill Villeneuve's place, was first to the flag.

The new Nürburgring staged the German Grand Prix in 1985. Since the 1950s sports cars had made few appearances at Hockenheim, but lacking the glories of the Grand Prix the circuit staged the German round of the World Endurance Championship over 1,000km. It was a day of blazing drama. The leading Porsche caught fire when being refuelled, the conflagration almost spreading to the whole pit area. Then another car burst into flames in the pits when its fuel tank leaked. Just before the end of the race a third fire started when fuel was spilt on a hot turbocharger.

Corrado Fabri's March 822 takes him to victory in the 1982 F2 Rhein-Pokalrennen.

The Ferrari F92As of Jean Alesi and Ivan Capelli run together in the early laps of the 1992 Grand Prix. Alesi is fifth but Capelli retired with a broken engine.

The Hockenheim circuit, 1970-2001.

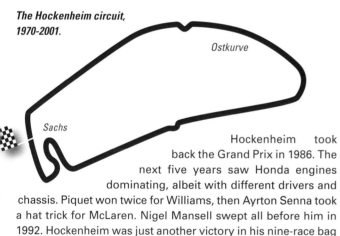

Hockenheim took back the Grand Prix in 1986. The next five years saw Honda engines dominating, albeit with different drivers and chassis. Piquet won twice for Williams, then Ayrton Senna took a hat trick for McLaren. Nigel Mansell swept all before him in 1992. Hockenheim was just another victory in his nine-race bag during his headlong rush to the Championship.

A collective red mist seemed to come down over half the grid at the start of the 1994 race. At the end of the first lap eleven cars were crumpled and battered in a series of multiple accidents and collisions. Fortunately no one was hurt. There was more drama when Jos Verstappen's Benneton caught fire at a pit stop. He and his crew were lucky to escape from the fireball with a singeing. Amid the chaos it was a good day for Ferrari, Gerhard Berger taking the flag to end a bleak four years without a Prancing Horse win.

The new star Michael Schumacher made a small piece of racing history the following year as the first German to win a

World Championship German Grand Prix. In 1999, with Schumacher sidelined after a crash in the British Grand Prix, Finland's Mika Salo was recruited by Ferrari to aid the team's Eddie Irvine toward the Championship. At Hockenhem Salo led the race then dutifully eased off to give the lead and victory to

A Ferrari takes the Ostschikane introduced to reduce speeds on the long Ostkurve for the 1992 Grand Prix.

Two Mercedes-Benzes lead the pack on the opening lap of the 1994 DTM round.

The Hockenheim crowds show their enthusiasm (or mania) for Michael Schumacher in 1995.

Far right: Michael Schumacher is acclaimed by the crowd even though he finishes second in the 1997 German Grand Prix. After the race he gives Giancarlo Fisichella, whose Jordan had retired, a lift back to the pits.

Below: These Mercedes are on the Stadium section of the circuit during the 2006 DTM round.

Irvine. After the race, Irvine presented the winner's trophy to Salo on the podium in gratitude.

In 2001 Schumacher, on his way to the World Championship, was punted at the Hockenheim start by a back marker. This was a race he didn't win, but it stayed in the family as the victor was brother Ralf.

At the end of the 2001 season there was a major circuit revamp by Bernie Ecclestone's favourite architect, Hermann Tilke. The long straights were unpopular with the team engineers, spectators and, most important of all, TV producers. The Stadium complex was retained, but after the beginning of the first long curve the track jinked right onto a new section cut through the forest. This joined the return leg and was followed by a right-hand bend and hairpin before coming back to the Stadium. The new circuit, now 2.8 miles (4.5km), had a clutch of additional grandstands and ideal TV viewing.

Michael Schumacher found Hockenheim's new layout to his liking. He took an easy win in 2002, repeating in 2004. New blood is always coming into the Grand Prix world, sometimes with exceptional talent. So it was in 2005 when Spain's Fernando Alonso burst onto the World Championship scene, challenging the existing stars in his Renault. Hockenheim was

Competing in the 2006 Deutsche Tourenwagen Meisterschaft (DTM) series, a Mercedes-Benz passes one of the vast grandstands built when Hockenheim underwent major reconstruction in 2002.

These competitors are on the stadium section of the Hockenheim circuit during the 2006 DTM round.

In spite of their racing modifications the 2008 DTM entries, like this Mercedes of Bernd Schneider, kept a semblance of stock-car appearance.

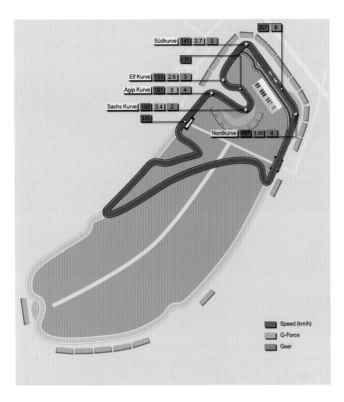

Südkurve 141 2.7 3

307 6

230

Elf Kurve 159 2.6 3

Agip Kurve 181 3 4

Sachs Kurve 100 2.4 2

335

Nordkurve 197 3.95 4

Speed (km/h)
G-Force
Gear

The current Hockenheim F1 circuit in grey.

one of the wins which took him to the 2005 Championship.

With seven Championship titles under his belt, Michael Schumacher had nothing left to prove. His last season (before his 2010 'unretirement') was to be 2006. Hockenheim was his last drive in front of his adoring German fans. He did not disappoint. Starting from the front row of the grid Michael took the lead after ten laps and went on to an untroubled win.

Politics hit Hockenheim in 2007. A dispute over the ownership of the

German Grand Prix title caused the race to be cancelled. The rival Nürburgring put on the European Grand Prix instead. It was decreed that henceforth the German title would alternate with the Ring.

Another new talent had taken the racing world by storm in 2007, Lewis Hamilton. He just missed the title in his rookie season but was well on target when he came to Hockenheim in 2008. He repaid the faith of his British fans by scoring a convincing win. There was German happiness too, for his McLaren had a Mercedes-Benz engine and proudly carried the three-pointed star.

In 2009, an alternate year, Hockenheim did not echo to the scream of Formula 1 engines. Its future may be uncertain; financial difficulties may curtail racing after 2010, but time will tell. Though inevitably overshadowed by the mighty Nürburgring and its legends, Hockenheim has been a valuable circuit. It has shown a readiness to move with the times and the changing needs of motor racing—though its essential character was lost with the 2001 changes.

MICHAEL SCHUMACHER

MICHAEL SCHUMACHER has the distinction of winning more World Championship races than any other driver. His tally of 91 victories may never be equalled. When he retired in 2006, it made his rivals' efforts look meagre.

Schumacher first raced in a Championship round at Hockenheim in 1992. Still in his first full F1 season, he took a Benetton-Ford into third place. It was a lucky podium finish, the third-place car obliging by spinning off with a lap to go. A year later history almost repeated itself with Schumacher one step higher on the podium. His Benetton was running third with a lap to go when second-place Damon Hill dropped out with a puncture.

In 1995 Michael Schumacher made a small piece of history as the first German driver to win a German Grand Prix in the post-1950 World Championship era. It was a convincing win. His Benetton powered by Renault led all the way apart from the fuel-stop laps. It was a decisive step to his first Championship.

Through the following years Schumacher won Championships as well as Championship rounds, though another win at Hockenheim eluded him. He scored places and had frustrating races from which he was eliminated by minor accidents.

In 2002 Michael was on his way to his fifth Championship. Arriving at Hockenheim, the title was almost his. He showed his mastery by leading from

flag to flag, interrupted only briefly by fuel stops. The critics called it boring, but the German crowd was ecstatic.

It was the same story in 2004. From pole position Schumacher took the lead at once. Pit stops gave his rivals the only chance to head the race. He cruised home. It was merely one of the thirteen wins that crushed his rivals that year, taking him to his fourth Championship.

The German crowd that came to Hockenheim in 2006 had heard rumours that Michael Schumacher would announce his retirement at the end of the season. If so, this would be the last chance for his German fans to see their hero in action on his home ground.

He didn't disappoint. After six laps Michael went past Kimi Raikkonen to take the lead. After that he was unchallenged. He was followed home by his Ferrari team-mate Felipe Massa. Massa was only 0.7sec behind as Schumacher took the flag, but it was a respectful second place. Massa would have risked a lynching from the partisan crowd if he'd passed their all-time hero.

The rumours were true. Schumacher retired at the end of 2006, but he left his German fans with the memory they wanted. He was good at that kind of thing. However, his racing days were not to end there. He returned in 2010 to the newly reformed Mercedes-Benz team. Perhaps more history will be made with an eighth title.

Lewis Hamilton is on the way to victory in the 2008 Grand Prix in his Mercedes-powered McLaren MP4/23.

On the podium Lewis Hamilton celebrates his 2008 German Grand Prix victory, one of the wins which secures him the Championship.

CHAPTER 17

Silverstone

Luigi Villoresi is flagged to his win in the 1948 Grand Prix in his Maserati 4CLT/48. Crowd control is minimal, the timekeepers use a caravan and the paddock is a field behind the pits where the transporters are parked.

*Right: **The huge crowd invades the course at the end of the 1948 Grand Prix while George Nixon, who comes tenth, pulls off into the paddock in his ERA. The only grandstand is a rudimentary construct of scaffolding and tarpaulins.***

IN the summer of 1942 bulldozers moved into the countryside, about five miles north of Buckingham, on the borders of Buckinghamshire and Northamptonshire. By May 1943 concrete and tarmac were laid and RAF Silverstone became an operational airfield. Although part of Bomber Command, Silverstone was the home of an Operational Training Unit where aircrews did their final training before going on 'ops'. Part of the training saw 40 Wellingtons of 17 OTU take part in minor raids on occupied France and later in diversionary raids to confuse German radar.

When World War 2 ended the RAF departed and Silverstone fell silent. In the immediate post-war years England had no racing circuits. Brooklands was no more, Donington was an army camp and the small track at Crystal Palace had reverted to a leisure park.

The RAC approached the Air Ministry, seeking the use of a disused airfield which could be used as a circuit. The Air Ministry was initially reluctant to help. After much negotiation it was agreed, in the summer of 1948, that Silverstone should be leased to the RAC. There was a proviso that there should be no permanent buildings so that it could revert to its former service use if necessary.

There had already been an unofficial race meeting at Silverstone. In September 1947 a group of Frazer Nash owners held an impromptu race on the perimeter track. There were no official results or any winners, but a sheep was killed by a car so the event became known as the 'Mutton Grand Prix'.

Wasting no time, on 2 October 1948 the RAC organised the first post-war British Grand Prix. A tortuous 3.7-mile

(5.9km) circuit was devised, marked out with straw bales, using the perimeter track and the centre runways. There was a hastily erected scaffold-supported grandstand with a row of board and scaffolding-pole pits. It drew an entry of all the top British drivers, most with obsolete cars, plus a handful of French and Italian racers. The Alfa Romeo team, which had dominated the 1948 season, was not persuaded to come.

Some 75,000 spectators saw an Italian Maserati win with veteran Luigi Villoresi taking the flag in front of his team-mate and protégé Alberto Ascari. The day began with a significant event, the first major race for the new 500cc class. These would become one of the launch pads for the British racing-car industry in the years to come.

The Grand Prix was run again in May 1949, this time nearly all on the perimeter track with a short runway excursion round a hairpin at Club Corner. The lap distance was 3.0 miles (4.8km). A slightly disappointing entry found the British racing against a second-division contingent of foreign drivers. It was

another Maserati win with Baron Emanuel de Graffenried of Switzerland at the wheel.

For British enthusiasts Silverstone was heaven-sent. It immediately became the home of club racing for the amateur. From 1949 to the present it has seen countless meetings for every type of car. For the first three seasons the club circuit used the main runway and the perimeter track from Copse to Stowe Corners. There were no facilities, the pits merely a row of straw bales.

Silverstone hit top gear in August 1949. The British Racing Drivers Club (BRDC) promoted the International Trophy meeting sponsored by the *Daily Express*. With all the top Grand Prix drivers present it was a win for Ascari's Ferrari. History was made as an XK120 Jaguar won the production-car race, launching a legend. Sadly the first fatality was Jock Horsfall, who was killed when his ERA overturned. It was significant, too, in that only the old perimeter track was used. This 2.9-mile (4.6km) course became the established circuit until 1974.

There was another 'first' in May 1950. Anointed with the 'European title', the British Grand Prix was the very first round in the new World Championship. It was attended by King George VI and Queen Elizabeth who saw an Alfa Romeo clean sweep. This was the only time a reigning monarch has watched a British motor race. Hopes were high for Britain's BRM, which made its first inauspicious racing appearance in the 1950 International Trophy. The legendary Tazio Nuvolari should have raced at this meeting with an XK120 Jaguar. He practised but withdrew, too ill to drive.

More history was made in 1951. The racing world had been waiting for the ever-improving Ferraris to topple the previously invincible Alfas. It happened at the British Grand Prix. The winning car was driven by Argentinean Froilan Gonzales, the 'Pampas Bull' who amazed and delighted the record crowd with his flamboyant style.

In the autumn of 1951 the BRDC bought the Silverstone lease from the RAC and instituted many improvements. The start was moved to the straight after Woodcote Corner and a row of permanent pits was built. Banks to give spectators a better view were made. The Club circuit was changed to run past the main pits, round Copse and Becketts Corners, then back along a runway behind the paddock to Woodcote.

Silverstone began to look more like a race circuit and less like an abandoned airfield. A pattern became established with the International Trophy in May, bringing top-class Grand Prix fields, followed by the Grand Prix in July. Both events had a full programme with supporting races for sports cars and saloons.

The 1954 Grand Prix saw the return of Mercedes-Benz to a British circuit. With unsuitable tyres on a moist track, Fangio's streamlined W196 was outrun by the Ferraris and Maseratis. It finished much dented by contact with the oil drums lining the corners. After that the drums went and the corners were lined with rows of breeze blocks. After a new circuit opened at Aintree, the Grand Prix went there in 1955. Thereafter it alternated between Aintree and Silverstone until 1962.

Since Silverstone opened its crowds had become accustomed to watching British cars at the rear of the field. Stirling Moss gave them something to cheer when his Vanwall

Raymond Sommer drives the V16 BRM at its ill-fated Silverstone debut in 1950.

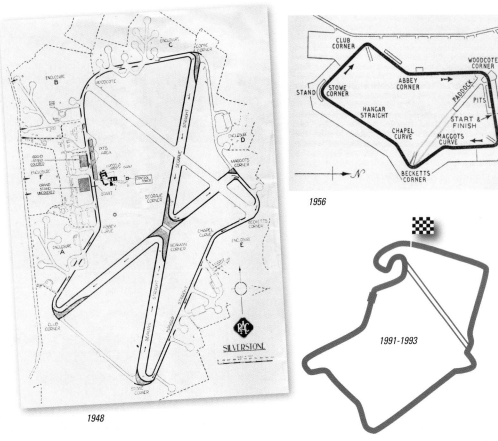

1948

SILVERSTONE – 1948 to present

1956

1991-1993

defeated Fangio's Ferrari in the 1956 International Trophy. It was a harbinger of future glories. The first British win in a Grand Prix at Silverstone came in 1960 when Jack Brabham's Cooper triumphed after Graham Hill's BRM had stormed through from last place to the lead, only to spin off within sight of the flag. Thereafter, except for a Matra success in 1969, no non-British car would be first to the flag in a Grand Prix at Silverstone until 1990.

Initially Silverstone had been dismissed by the top Grand Prix drivers as an 'in-between circuit', neither slow nor especially fast. With minor improvement and a better surface, however, speeds were increasing. It was gradually moving into the ranks of the fast circuits, joining venues such as Spa and Monza. The speed with which the cars were taking Woodcote Corner, and a tragic accident to an official standing in front of the pits at the 1963 Grand Prix, prompted changes. A separate elevated pit road was built for the 1964 season.

Aintree had dropped out of the frame and the Grand Prix now alternated between Silverstone and Brands Hatch. One of the greatest of all, Jim Clark, scored a hat trick of

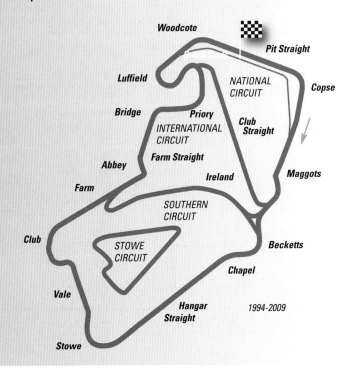

1994-2009

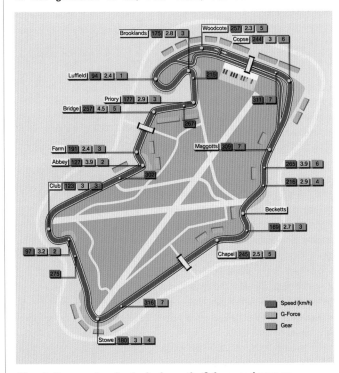

Circuit diagram showing typical speeds, G-force and gear as used in F1 in 2002.

Louis Rosier takes Stowe Corner with his Lago-Talbot in the 1949 Grand Prix. He comes third.

Swiss Baron 'Toulo' de Graffenreid wins the 1949 Grand Prix in a Maserati 4CLT/48 'San Remo'.

Froilan Gonzales throws his Ferrari 375 F1 around with abandon while winning the 1951 Grand Prix, ending an era of Alfa Romeo dominance of Grand Prix racing.

Piero Taruffi aims his Ferrari 500 F2 into Abbey Curve in the 1952 Grand Prix. He places second behind his team-mate Alberto Ascari.

Silverstone wins in 1963, 1965 and 1967. His green Lotus with its yellow stripe was unbeatable. Amidst the excitement of the big meetings, the club circuit was seeing action every weekend from early spring until late autumn.

The development of the Formula 1 car had been rapid. In the 1973 Grand Prix the fastest lap was 134.06mph (215.70km/h). The 1973 race saw high drama. On the opening lap South African Jody Scheckter spun his McLaren exiting Woodcote. In the ensuing chaos eight cars were eliminated and the race had to be restarted.

With the changing face of Formula 1, the importance of the International Trophy diminished. It was still useful to teams for early-season testing, but fields had to be made up with Formula 5000 cars. The Duke of Edinburgh attended the 1974 Trophy. He opened a new pit garage complex, intended to give the Formula 1 teams the facilities now expected.

Aimed at reducing the speed of cars through Woodcote, entering the pit straight, the line of the corner was changed in 1975 to make a gentle chicane. It made little difference; within a year the cars were lapping at the same speeds as before.

The RAC Tourist Trophy is Britain's oldest race, instituted in 1906. It came to Silverstone in 1970. Run as a touring-car event, it drew big and competitive fields. The series continued annually until 1988 when the TT moved to Donington. The next

The Maserati A6GCM of Gonzales is scrutineered before the 1953 Grand Prix. The paddock is then the runway behind the pits with the scrutineering bay under a temporary canvas awning.

Far right: **At the start of the 1953 Grand Prix, Gonzales (Maserati A6GCM No 22) just heads eventual winner Ascari (Ferrari 500 F2 No 5) while Hawthorn (Ferrari 500 F2 No 8) looks across and feels for the gear lever.**

refugee to find a Silverstone sanctuary was the British round of the World Sports Car Championship in 1976, run as a six-hour race. In 1980 a woman driver took the chequered flag, Desireé Wilson sharing the wheel of the winning De Cadenet-Lola.

After alternating with Brands Hatch, the British Grand Prix came to rest at Silverstone in 1987. It delivered a momentous race. With this the era of the turbochargers in Formula 1, the BRDC put in a new chicane before the entry to Woodcote to

Mike Hawthorn sprints away into the lead at the start of the 1956 British Grand Prix. He has an unhappy race as his BRM P25 retires with an oil leak.

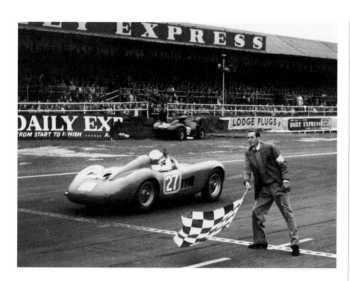

slow the powerful cars. It made no difference. By the time the cars passed the pits they were doing 190mph (305km/h).

Briton Nigel Mansell regarded Silverstone as his home track and desperately wanted to win. He trailed Williams teammate Nelson Piquet for 63 laps, then with an audacious passing manoeuvre at Stowe took the lead and then the flag two laps later. It was close, as Mansell ran out of fuel on the slowing-down lap. During the race Mansell lapped at the incredible speed of 153.06mph (246.27km/h). Truly Silverstone was one of the fastest.

Speed anxieties were allayed in 1988 as the Grand Prix was run in heavy rain, allowing Ayrton Senna to show his mastery. In the dry, during the next two years, it was up to pace again. The BRDC took drastic action. It built a new series of curves, cutting out Becketts. At the end of the Hangar Straight, instead of taking a rapid Stowe corner, the cars curved round onto a new section, Vale, which led to an ess-bend at Club Corner. Going uphill round Abbey curve, the cars entered a new complex of four corners named Priory and Luffield before going onto the pit straight. The changes increased the lap distance to 3.2 miles (5.2km). A variety of minor circuits were laid out for club events, testing and training.

Mansell, 'Our Nige' to his countrymen, did it again on the new circuit in 1991. His closest rival, Senna, ran out of fuel with two laps to go. During the slowing-down lap Mansell picked him up and gave him a lift back to the pits, sitting on the side pod of the Williams. In 1992 Mansell was en route to the Championship and scored again. The crowds erupted onto the track to acclaim him at the end of the race.

Alain Prost deserved the nickname of 'The Professor' with his clinical approach to his racing. In 1993 he scored an easy win in his Williams-Renault, ahead of new boy Michael Schumacher. It was Prost's fifth GP win on the circuit. He had already scored in 1982, 1985, 1989 and 1990. In term of wins, Prost has been the most successful driver in the British Grands Prix held on the circuit.

The 1994 race brought an outcome of satisfying sentiment. Despite gaining two World Championships Graham Hill had never taken the Silverstone race, but his son Damon secured the win in a Williams to the huge delight of the ever-partisan crowd. A year later there was more sentimental satisfaction for the crowd. Horrific injuries in a crash had nearly ended Johnny Herbert's career in 1988 but he took an unexpected win in the 1995 Grand Prix in a Benetton-Renault.

The Schumacher years had begun. His red Ferrari took the 1998 race, but there was near-disaster when he crashed in 1999 and his broken leg kept him out for most of the season. It was Schumacher again in 2002, then the turn of his Ferrari teammate Rubens Barrichello in 2003. It was a bizarre race, as an Irish priest ran onto the track during the race, waving a placard. The safety car came out until he was restrained.

While the British Grand Prix was the big attraction at Silverstone, the 1,000km for sports cars drew the major manufacturers each year. Between 1983 and 1988 the spoils were shared between Porsche and Jaguar. In 1990 the race distance was cut to 500km. After a lull between 1993 and 2003 the full 1,000km race was restored as a round in the Le Mans Endurance Series.

By the early years of the 21st century, Silverstone had grown from a primitive airfield to the ranks of the senior circuits. Only Monza, Spa, Monaco and the Nürburgring had a longer history, the German circuit bearing little relationship to

Passing the pits in his Cooper-Climax Type 45 in the 1958 BRDC International Trophy, Stirling Moss is out of luck, retiring with a broken gearbox.

Top left: Stirling Moss takes the flag in a Maserati 300S to win the supporting sports-car race at the 1956 Grand Prix.

NIGEL MANSELL

NIGEL MANSELL has a special place in the affections of British race followers. His tough, no-compromise attitude, his battle to rise to the top and his recovery from near-fatal injuries won him many admirers. After the golden years of the 1960s and early 1970s and the brief flowering of James Hunt, by 1980 British participants in the World Championship lurked at the back of the grid. Mansell put British driving back at the front with wins in Championship rounds in 1985. In 1986 Nigel was Championship runner-up, having taken the British Grand Prix at Brands Hatch.

The fans who came to Silverstone in 1987 hoped to see a British driver win the premier national race in a British car. Mansell was in a turbo-powered Williams-Honda with Nelson Piquet his team-mate. The two Williams were the fastest cars in the field. Their strategy was to run non-stop, but at half distance Mansell had to pit to change a vibrating wheel. He set off in pursuit of Piquet, disdaining the all-important constraints on fuel consumption. With three laps to go he caught Piquet, jinking into the lead despite the Brazilian's blocking tactics. Mansell took the flag to huge acclamation. It had been too close for comfort: he ran out of fuel on the slowing-down lap.

The British Grand Prix had come to rest at Silverstone, where Mansell could only manage a second place in 1988 in an off-pace Williams. The fans forgave his move to Ferrari in 1989 and 1990. A puncture probably prevented a win in 1989.

In 1991 'Mansell Mania' gripped the crowds. The feisty Brummie had become their hero. At the start Mansell's Williams-Renault was outpaced by Senna's McLaren-Honda. Half-way round the first lap, Mansell pushed to the front. To the delight of the crowd he motored away to the flag. Senna, who had pursued all the way, ran out of fuel on the last lap. Mansell slowed on the lap of honour and gave Senna a lift back to the pits, sitting on the side pod of the Williams.

'Mansell Mania' reached new heights in 1992 when 'Our Nige' won six of the first eight points-scoring rounds, The Champion's laurels were almost resting on his brow when the teams came to Silverstone. Mansell and his team-mate Riccardo Patrese dominated the race. The two Williams-Renaults led from flag to flag, Mansell coming home with a comfortable 39-second advantage. This time the crowd erupted onto the track in a scene more reminiscent of Monza than reserved British Silverstone. Mansell and his car were mobbed and he had to be rescued by marshals. He went on to take the Championship with ease. It was his last Formula 1 drive in front of his adoring home fans.

its majestic first incarnation. Changes have been made to the lines of Luffield and Copse corners, but despite these it is still one of the fastest circuits.

At the time of writing cars lap at speeds approaching 145mph (235km/h). Silverstone is respected by the top drivers, who say it is one of the most challenging and rewarding circuits of all, especially over the section from the start line to Hangar Straight.

A major difficulty was partially overcome in 2002. There had been traffic snarl-ups around the circuit, which was approached by narrow lanes. This was allayed when a major link road was built between the M1 and M40, joined by a four-lane road from the circuit. Getting out of the circuit on race days still remains a problem.

In 2006 the Silverstone race was a stepping stone for Renault ace Fernando Alonso on his way to the Championship. A pattern was established when Ferrari's Finn, Kimi Räikkönen, took a convincing 2007 win as he too went on to be Champion.

For British fans 2008 was a return to the ecstasy of the Mansell years. Lewis Hamilton had become the national hero. Pouring rain did nothing to dampen his skills or the joy of the crowd when he took his McLaren-Mercedes to a dominating win with a margin of 68 seconds, the biggest in any World Championship round for 13 years. Hamilton also went on to Championship glory. In 2009 the patriotic crowds hoped to cheer ultimate Championship winner Jenson Button to victory, so there was muted enthusiasm when German Sebastian Vettel took the flag.

Silverstone has earned its place as the national home of British motor sport. The adjoining industrial estate is the base of some Formula 1 teams and many firms in the motor racing industry. Throughout the year, countless events on its variety of circuits range from races for karts and vintage cars to championship touring cars.

It was a bitter blow for the BRDC and for all enthusiasts when F1 boss Bernie Ecclestone announced that Silverstone's facilities did not match up to the most modern circuits. The British Grand Prix would move to Donington in 2010. In December 2009, Silverstone was granted a reprieve as the lessees of Donington were unable to meet their contractual obligations. Silverstone was awarded a new contract to host the British Grand Prix for 17 seasons. It is a term of the contract that there will be major improvements and alterations. Silverstone will always have a special place in the hearts of British enthusiasts. Its future now seems assured.

Left: Ronnie Peterson's Lotus 72 leads Jackie Stewart's Tyrrell 006 in the early laps after the re-start of the 1973 Grand Prix. Peterson finished second.

Gilles Villeneuve held third place for three laps in his Ferrari 126CK in the 1981 Grand Prix, then hit the kerb at Woodcote, spun and crashed out of the race.

This Harrods-sponsored McLaren F1 GTR takes Andy Wallace and Olivier Grouillard to victory in the 1995 Silverstone Four Hours, a round in the Global Endurance Series.

Reigning champion Lewis Hamilton has an unhappy home Grand Prix in 2009, finishing 16th with his McLaren MP4/24 after leaving the track several times.

CHAPTER 18

Brands Hatch

Stirling Moss takes the flag in his Cooper-JAP at a 500cc meeting in June 1950. Races are run in an anti-clockwise direction until 1954. The edges of the track are rough and ill-defined in the early years.

In August 1954 the Daily Telegraph Trophy, a major 500cc race, gets under way. The Club circuit made a natural arena for the spectators.

BRANDS HATCH — 'Brands', as it is colloquially known — is probably the most-used circuit in Britain and perhaps in the world. It all began in the 1920s.

On an outing in 1926 some bicycle-club members saw a sloping field adjoining the London-Dover A20 highway. The owner, a local farmer, let them use the field for races and time trials. In 1928 motorcycles moved in, a kidney-shaped grass track was laid out and three local motorcycle clubs formed a combine to promote races.

These events prospered. By the start of World War 2 Brands had become a major grass-track racing venue. A regular competitor was Jack Surtees, who brought his young son John to watch the racing. There had been tentative proposals in 1938 to tarmac the course and make it suitable for cars. During World War 2 the Army moved in, but unlike Donington it left when the war ended.

Motorcycle racing soon resumed. In 1947 Brands Hatch Stadium, Ltd. was formed to manage the embryo circuit. One rider competing in the grass-track races was Bernie Ecclestone, then 17 years old. In 1949 a youthful and ambitious Ecclestone tried to buy the track, but negotiations fell through. A welcome injection of new blood came into motor racing in the immediate post-war years with the appearance of the 500cc class. Aimed at the more impecunious enthusiast, it used motorcycle engines. Within a year it became a fiercely contested class using relatively sophisticated series-production cars. At the beginning of 1950 it was recognised by the FIA as Formula 3.

In 1949 the Half-Litre Club, the moving force behind 500cc racing, persuaded Brands Hatch Stadium that the 1938 plan should be implemented. A tarmac surface was laid on the existing grass-track course. After a motorcycle meeting was held in March 1950, the Half-Litre Club promoted the first car meeting on 16 April with a programme devoted wholly to 500s. The winner of the first race was Don Parker driving his Parker-CFS.

Six more meetings were held during the 1950 season with an international meeting in August. The racing was close and popular with the crowds who could see all the circuit from the enclosures. The cars raced anti-clockwise so some of the lower-powered 500s found the climb up Paddock Hill to be demanding.

New drivers were emerging. Young Bernie Ecclestone had several wins while among the motorcyclists a remarkable talent, John Surtees, was soon dominating. The 1950 August international meeting secured sponsorship from the *Daily Telegraph*. Half-litre racing continued in 1951, 1952 and 1953. Some fatalities showed that Brands was an unforgiving circuit which punished drivers' mistakes.

The Half-Litre Club was ambitious. Grasping that 500cc racing had already seen its best seasons, it decided to support the rapidly growing small-capacity sports-car classes typified by the embryonic Lotus. This decision coincided with another conclusion: that Brands should be extended. A new loop was

A Formula 1 field came to Brands for the first time in October 1956. In a 15-lap race Roy Salvadori's Maserati 250F leads Archie Scott-Brown's Connaught B-Type into Druids. Scott-Brown goes on to win with Salvadori third.

built from the bottom of Paddock Hill that ascended the hill, rounded a hairpin, Druids, and went back downhill to rejoin the original circuit. This increased the lap distance to 1.25 miles (2.0km). In future cars would race in a clockwise direction. The first meeting on the new circuit, for sports cars and 500s, was held at Easter 1954.

The Half-Litre Club had become the British Racing & Sports Car Club (BRSCC) in 1954, an outfit that showed imagination. The August Bank Holiday meeting became a major sports-car event. A remarkable and successful innovation was a Boxing Day meeting, the day after Christmas, which pulled in large crowds.

The 1956 August meeting saw one of the first races for the 1.5-litre Formula 2 that took official effect in 1957. Another F2 race in the 1956 October meeting was won by a new name, Tony Brooks, who duelled with Jack Brabham for several laps. The October meeting had an exciting innovation, a portent of the future: a Formula 1 race. It drew a small field for a 15-lap contest in which the Connaught works team fought off private

entrants with victory going to the remarkable disabled driver Archie Scott-Brown.

There were ambitious plans for the future. In the mid-1950s the woods to the south of the track behind Druids Bend were bulldozed and the trees cleared for access to a major extension. There was no money to complete the plans at that time. Brands was still crude. There were no proper pits and the paddock was a cinder track with an ancient wooden clubhouse and café. A small permanent grandstand had been bought from a defunct horse-racing track and erected opposite the start line.

Other clubs organised races and sprints, keeping the circuit in action almost every weekend. It was open for testing during the week and for race-driving schools that were established, notably by Coopers. The Formula 2 races were the attraction at the major meetings and every driver of note appeared.

Brands was still a minor circuit on the international scene. During the winter of 1959-60 it jumped into the top league.

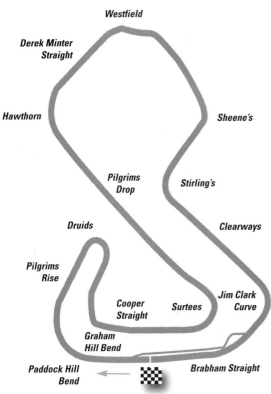

Westfield

Derek Minter
Straight

Hawthorn

Sheene's

Pilgrims
Drop

Stirling's

Druids

Clearways

Pilgrims
Rise

Cooper
Straight

Surtees

Jim Clark
Curve

Graham
Hill Bend

Paddock Hill
Bend

Brabham Straight

Dennis Taylor with a Lotus 12 leads New Zealand driver Syd Jensen with a Cooper Type 45 round Druids in a Formula 2 race in June 1958. Jensen is followed by the Cooper 45 of a youthful Bruce McLaren.

Two Jaguars are chased by an Austin A40 in a 1960 saloon-car race.

Jim Clark leads all the way with his Lotus 25 in the 1964 British Grand Prix. He is trailed throughout by Graham Hill's BRM, which is in the background.

The cleared sections in the woods were surfaced, extending the circuit to 2.65 miles (4.26km). With its fast, swooping bends running through woodland, the extension had some aspects reminiscent of the old Nürburgring.

A permanent pit complex was built in the centre of the original circuit with a multi-storey control tower. The grandstand was extended. The paddock was surfaced and partially levelled. The extended circuit became known as the Grand Prix circuit while the short original track became the Club circuit.

A Formula 1 race, the Silver City Trophy, was run over the extended track in August 1960. Drawing a field of World Championship quality, it was won by Jack Brabham whose Cooper was chased home by Graham Hill's BRM. Repeated in 1961, it saw a win for Stirling Moss. The Club circuit was hosting daily action with testing, demonstrations and racing every weekend with motorcycles or cars. Another move up the ladder came in 1962 with the longest race yet on the circuit, a six-hour saloon-car event.

Ownership of the circuit changed in 1961 when it was bought by Grovewood Securities, which put money into the circuit, making many improvements to the facilities. John Webb, who had handled the circuit's publicity since 1954, brokered the deal. He was appointed as a director of Grovewood and circuit manager. Though Webb was not universally popular, his drive, ambition and imagination would make Brands a world-calibre track.

Since 1955 the British Grand Prix had alternated between Silverstone and Aintree. After negotiations lasting more than a year, the RAC agreed that the 1964 Grand Prix would be held at Brands. The circuit had climbed to the top of the tree. A combined RAC/BRSCC organisation staged the meeting, with the Grand Prix going to Jim Clark's Lotus, pursued all the way by Graham Hill's BRM. In third place with a Ferrari was local hero John Surtees.

In 1965, the BRSCC instituted the non-Championship Formula 1 Race of Champions. This gave an early season outing for the major teams in the non-Grand Prix years at Brands. It became a regular fixture. The 1965 race saw Jim Clark make an uncharacteristic error and crash out in his Lotus. Another innovation was the Guards 1,000 mile race for production sports cars. Run over two days with two 500-mile heats, the result was found on aggregate times.

The British Grand Prix was back in 1966. Among the track's many improvements was construction of 100 covered paddock bays. Promoted as 'The Return to Power', 1966 was the first year of the 3.0-litre formula. The race was a *tour de force* for the Brabham team. Driver/constructor Jack won, followed home by team-mate Denny 'The Bear' Hulme. During the meeting filming was done for the movie *Grand Prix*, including staged races for mock-up Formula 1 cars.

The Stars and Stripes waved at Brands in 1967. The Race of Champions went to American Dan Gurney in his Eagle-Weslake. Engine-builder Harry Weslake was as pleased as Gurney with the 100 bottles of champagne the driver won with his pole-position practice lap. The BOAC 500, a round in the Championship of Makes, saw a win for the unorthodox Chaparral driven by ex-champion Phil Hill with Mike Spence. This was the final race victory for the popular Hill.

A pattern was now established with the Grand Prix coming to Brands in alternate years, and the Race of Champions had an annual season-setting fixture. The BOAC 500 was also in the calendar as a round of the sports-car

Ian Raby (Brabham BT3 No 21) and Richard Attwood (Lotus 25 No 18) lead the tail-enders round Paddock Hill Bend after the start of the 1965 Race of Champions.

The technically advanced and unorthodox Chaparral takes Mike Spence and 1961 World Champion Phil Hill to victory in the 1967 Six Hours. Hill retires after this success.

Championship of Makes. Long-distance touring cars were back for the Guards Six Hours, the British round in the European Touring Car Championship.

Some races become a legend in the sport. Brands contributed one in April of 1970 at the BOAC 1,000 Km. In relentless rain a titanic battle was fought between the Ferrari and Porsche teams, neither side yielding. The ultimate winner was a Gulf-sponsored Porsche 917 driven chiefly by Pedro Rodriguez. Those who watched him in action that day still speak of the Mexican's drive in awe.

A major tragedy marred the end of the 1971 season. In the non-Championship Formula One Victory Race, Swiss driver Jo Siffert — winner of the 1968 British Grand Prix — went off the track in his BRM and died when it caught fire. Subsequently there was criticism of the circuit and its safety arrangements. Much remedial work was done, especially on the Grand Prix loop.

Although 68,000 came to Brands to watch Jody Scheckter win the 1974 British Grand Prix in a Tyrrell, the British Airways 1,000, a Makes Championship round, drew only a meagre 7,000. Perhaps the motor racing public was becoming more discerning or perhaps there was too much racing. Meanwhile big things were happening alongside the circuit. The M20 motorway was being built adjacent to the paddock entrance road. This allowed much-needed improvements to the paddock, part of which was on a hillside, while new pits met the demands of the Formula 1 teams.

The revamped circuit was ready for 1976 and a controversial Grand Prix. James Hunt and Clay Regazzoni were involved in a first-lap collision at Paddock Hill Bend. After the race was stopped, both teams worked furiously to repair their respective McLaren and Ferrari for the re-start. When it was

The field waits for the flag in the 1970 Race of Champions. On the back row are the Lotus 49 of American Pete Lovely and the BRM 153 of Canadian George Eaton.

announced that neither would be allowed to restart as they hadn't completed the first red-flag lap, the crowd grew menacing at the prospect of their hero Hunt being excluded.

Bending to *force majeure*, fearing a riot, the stewards allowed both to race. With Hunt's win it should have been a fairy-tale ending, but after the race — and after the crowds had dispersed — it was decreed that the rules had been broken and Hunt was disqualified. Though Niki Lauda was the surprised beneficiary, Hunt pipped him to the World Championship by a single point that year.

At Easter 1980 a small piece of history was made at Brands when Desirée Wilson won the Formula 1 Evening News Trophy. Though it was a minor race, she became the first — and so far only — woman to win a Formula 1 event. Brands had become a venue for rallycross, using sections of the circuit, the infield and the car parks. The first British Rallycross GP was held there in 1982. That year's British Grand Prix saw Niki Lauda take the flag in a McLaren. At the end of the season the

Formula One Constructors' Association awarded Brands the prize for the best Grand Prix of 1982.

Formula 1 was evolving. With major teams opting to compete only in Championship rounds, the non-Championship

The field gets away in the 1969 Race of Champions. Jo Siffert's Lotus 49 (No 20) is in the centre and Bruce McLaren in an M7A (No 4) is on the right. The exaggerated high wings are soon banned.

Nigel Mansell in a Williams FW10 (No 5) is about to wrest the lead from Ayrton Senna (Lotus 97T No 12) at Druids in the 1985 European Grand Prix. Mansell went on to win and Senna was second.

races were fading away. The last Race of Champions was in 1983. Despite this, Brands was flying high. When two Championship rounds were cancelled, Webb and his team were invited to organise an European Grand Prix to fill the gap in the 1983 calendar. It was a big success with a win for Nelson Piquet in a Brabham-BMW.

The British Grand Prix was back again in 1984. The race was red-flagged and restarted after Dr. Jonathan Palmer, who had abandoned medicine for motor racing, crashed his Hart-powered RAM. Lauda won again, but Palmer would be back at Brands in a different role. The European Grand Prix was run again in 1985. It saw Nigel Mansell take his first Championship win in a Williams. Mansell had raced a Formula Ford at Brands in 1976 and 1977. In the latter year an accident at the circuit had almost brought his budding career to an end.

Mansell had a lucky win in the 1986 Grand Prix. His transmission broke on the grid, seemingly retiring him. After a first-lap accident, however, the race was restarted and his car was repaired in time. It was the last Grand Prix to be staged at Brands.

In 1972 track owner Grovewood had been acquired by Eagle Star. In 1986 Eagle Star decided to sell Brands Hatch and its operating company. The outcome was clouded by politics, ambition and a measure of wounded pride. Bernie Ecclestone

decided to give the Grand Prix to Silverstone indefinitely. When the dust settled the new owner of the track was John Foulston, one of the new breed of computer tycoons.

The loss of the Grand Prix made little difference. Thanks to its nearness to London, Brands still lived up to the title of 'the busiest racing circuit in the World', offering a succession of meetings for every type of racing. Foulston's ownership was short-lived as he was killed in a racing accident at Silverstone in September 1987. His wife took over the reins of the management company.

The track gained royal patronage in July 1988 when HRH The Prince of Wales attended a car festival in aid of the Prince's Trust. The Prince drove round the circuit in a 1930 Bentley, togged in a crash helmet adorned with his three-feathered crest. The Brands 1,000 Km offered a fierce battle between the Jaguar and Sauber-Mercedes teams, ending in a British win. Changes made to the Grand Prix loop included a chicane at Dingle Dell and the realignment of Westfield corner. At the end of 1989 circuit chief John Webb retired and Nicola, Foulston's ambitious 21-year-old daughter, took over control.

Under Nicola Foulston the character of racing at Brands changed, minor club events being abandoned. Brands Hatch was floated as a public company, helping fund a new pits complex in 1995. Instead of long-distance events the fare on

NIKI LAUDA

Niki Lauda brought a new dimension of courage to Formula 1. After winning the World title in 1975, a fiery crash at the Nürburgring almost cost him his life and left him with disfiguring scars. He came back to win two more Championships.

Lauda came to Brands in 1976 as Champion. That year's British Grand Prix was an unhappy race. A first-lap crash involved several drivers including James Hunt. Hunt took the restart and apparently won, but months later the authorities ruled he shouldn't have been allowed to start again. The race was awarded to Lauda, whose Ferrari came second on the road after being passed by Hunt at half distance.

Two weeks later Lauda had his crash at the Ring. A recovering Niki took the World Championship in 1977. He was back at Brands in 1978 with a heavy and unbiddable Brabham-Alfa. Out-fumbled by Carlos Reutemann in a Ferrari when they were lapping a back marker, he lost the race by a mere 1.3 seconds. To general surprise a disillusioned Lauda walked away from the sport at the end of 1979.

For two years Lauda built up his business interests. Then in 1982 he was lured back by the wiles of McLaren's Ron Dennis and Marlboro's money. With the Woking team he showed that none of his former pace had gone.

He took on a rigorous regime to restore his fitness.

In the 1982 British Grand Prix at Brands Niki started from the fourth row of the grid. The car in front of him had been relegated to the rear so Lauda had a clear run. By the first corner he was second behind Piquet. He stayed there until Piquet dropped out after nine laps, then went on to win easily. He eased off at the end, even letting some drivers unlap themselves. The old Lauda form was back.

In 1984 the Grand Prix at Brands drew 90,000 spectators. The leaders had to dodge the melee of a first-lap crash involving four cars. Lauda, still McLaren-mounted, was running third. Another crash after nine laps stopped the race. At the restart Lauda ran third again. He moved ahead of Piquet and began chasing Alain Prost. The race fell into Lauda's lap. Prost stopped with a broken gearbox and Piquet gave up his chase of Lauda when his turbo failed. This left Lauda cruising home to another Brands win. When the times of the two parts were aggregated Niki Lauda came out on top with a 42-second advantage. The Brands Hatch win was a prelude to Lauda's third World Championship. He finally retired at the end of 1985.

offer was short races, emphasising Formula Ford, Formula 3 and touring cars. Nicola Foulston stepped back in 2001 and Octagon took over the circuit management until 2004. Plans were announced for the return of the Grand Prix with massive changes to the track. This all fell through.

In 2004 Brands was bought by Motorsport Vision, a company masterminded by Jonathan Palmer. Since then Palmer has backed a programme of continuous improvement. Versatile and viewable, the track continued to provide a massive calendar of events each year, holding a vital place in British motor racing. Though Brands has probably seen its greatest glories, it has a unique hold on the affections of all British enthusiasts which it is likely to maintain for years to come.

Right: **The field leaves the grid for a Renault Clio Cup race in 2007. Such one-make series have featured regularly at Brands for many years.**

A Mercedes-Benz leads the pack at Paddock Hill Bend in a round of the 2009 DTM Championship.

CHAPTER 19

Imola

Luigi Musso in a Maserati A6GCS/2000 is in front at the start of the 1954 Imola Grand Prix. Eventual winner Umberto Maglioli in a Ferrari Mondial 2000 (No 36) takes an inside line.

JUST as Hockenheim will always be linked with Jim Clark, so Imola is linked to Ayrton Senna for the same tragic reason. The weekend of 30 April/1 May 1994 offered the Formula 1 circus unrelenting horror. During practice for the San Marino Grand Prix, Austrian rookie Roland Ratzenberger crashed his Simtek-Ford and was killed. Then the following day, on the sixth lap of the Grand Prix, three-times World Champion Ayrton Senna left the road in his Williams-Renault, struck a wall and was killed by a piece of debris from his car which penetrated his helmet. It was Formula 1's blackest weekend for 34 years.

The Imola track, the scene of these disasters, had opened 40 years earlier. It was the brainchild of local enthusiasts who realised that Maserati and Ferrari in nearby Modena and Maranello needed a test track nearer home than Monza. A 3.14-mile (5.06km) circuit was planned using roads in the local undulating Castellaccio Park. It was a picturesque site with

a nearby river and overlooked by a church. After an initial meeting for motorcycles, the cars came in June 1954.

The debut race was the Grand Prix di Imola sponsored by oil giant Shell. A 2.0-litre sports-car race, it pulled a field of Italian drivers, some from Formula 1, with Ferrari and Maserati works entries. The winner was Ferrari pilot Umberto Maglioli. When the GP was run again in 1955 Maserati took the prize, with Cesare Perdisa leading Maglioli home. When in 1956 the category was changed to move down a class to 1.5-litre sports-racers, Jack Brabham took a 'bob-tail' Cooper all the way from England to finish second behind Eugenio Castellotti's Osca.

Thereafter Imola saw testing, motorcycles and minor events until 1963, when it moved up to the fringes of the big time. In April of 1963 the Formula 1 circus rolled into town for the non-Championship GP Citta di Imola. Among the runners in a second-division entry were Team Lotus green-and-yellow Lotus 25s, state-of-the-art machines driven by Jim Clark and Trevor Taylor. The flag fell and Clark disappeared into the distance, only seen by the rest of the field as he lapped them. It was a foretaste of the rest of Clark's season when he took his first Championship. Though it would take 16 years for Formula 1 to return to Imola, in the meantime there was regular action as well as Ferrari testing.

France's Guy Ligier, soon to become a Formula 1 driver, entrant and constructor, took a GT race at Imola with a Porsche in 1964. In Imola's annual Formula 3 fixtures were names soon to become familiar in the higher echelons. In 1968 a 500km sports-car race, at the end of the season, pulled in all the major teams and witnessed wins for Alfa Romeo, Mirage and Porsche. The 1970 race saw a fight between the awesome 917 Porsches and Ferrari 512s with background music supplied by thunderous Lola-Chevrolets. The 1.6-litre Formula 2 became a major force with all the leading drivers competing. It came to Imola in 1970 when a fifth of a second covered the first three finishers after a race-long fight in the GP Citta di Imola.

The grid forms up for the
Shell Gold Cup in 1957.
At that time the circuit was
less developed.

Start of a Formula 3 race in
1966.

British multi-World-
Champion Phil Read takes
Tosa Corner on a 250cc
Yamaha in 1966.

159

During this bitter battle between Ferrari team-mates Gilles Villeneuve and Didier Pironi, in the 1982 San Marino Grand Prix, Pironi refuses to obey team orders and passes Villeneuve to win.

The Formula 2 and 500km races continued. Then in 1974 Imola moved a rung up the ladder with a 1,000-km round of the Sports Car Championship. Ferrari was concentrating on Formula 1, so the *tifosi* had to cheer for Alfa Romeo instead. At the finish cheers were muted as the flag fell for the blue French Matra.

The track had become the Autodromo Dino Ferrari in memory of Enzo's son Alfredo 'Dino', who had died in 1958. The Sports Car Championship missed Imola in 1975 but was back in 1976. It should have been a Renault-Alpine win, but the hopes of both the French team and the Italians were frustrated by a Porsche victory. Imola was still a Championship round in 1977 but reduced to a mere 250km sprint, won by an Alfa. Bigger days were coming, though.

Politics brought good news to Imola's promoters. Italy wanted to hold two World Championship rounds, needing another venue to back up the legendary Italian Grand Prix at Monza. While FISA had been willing to grant a country the peripatetic European GP to back up their annual national race, it turned its face against a country running two Championship rounds every year. What was the solution?

Italy's sporting authority, the Commissione Sportiva Automobilistica Italiana, had a brain wave. The little enclave of San Marino, near the Adriatic coastal resort of Rimini, had population of a mere 20,000 but was an independent republic. Though effectively a part of Italy, it had much the same relationship as Monaco bore to France. Of course San Marino

should have a national Grand Prix! With no space for a circuit in the minuscule republic, it would be held at Imola.

A secondary reason for anointing Imola was that dissatisfaction had arisen with Monza and its safety arrangements. Imola could be an alternative venue for the Italian GP While negotiations over the 'San Marino' idea proceeded, a non-Championship race was held at Imola near the end of the 1979 season. The GP di Dino Ferrari drew entries from all the major teams and the result satisfied the Italian fans. Though a Ferrari didn't win, a Brabham did — with an Alfa Romeo engine. Monza was told to clean up its act and the Italian GP did indeed go to Imola in 1980. Some corners were revised with chicanes which increased the lap distance by 175yd (160m), though this made little difference to lap times. The first Championship round at Imola went poorly for the home teams. Ferrari was having a lean season and Alfa Romeo was in disarray. Neither featured in the results. The race went to Brazilian Nelson Piquet in a Brabham while Australian Alan Jones, on his way to the 1980 Championship, came second in a Williams.

Successful revisions to Monza allowed the Italian GP to return there in 1981. With the drivers enjoying Imola and Italian desires satisfied by the additional race, the San Marino GP was posted in the 1981 calendar as a Championship round. Run in May, it became established as the first European round after the flyaway races. Piquet won again, the second of three wins which would give him the Championship by a single point at the end of the season.

The 1982 began with several teams in dispute with FISA over regulations, especially the weight of cars. When it came to a head the week before the Imola race, several teams withdrew. Ferrari kept faith with its *tifosi* and competed. The result was a Ferrari one-two that fuelled dissension in the Maranello camp. In the closing laps for the Ferrari pair Gilles Villeneuve was leading Didier Pironi, both having a commanding lead over the rest of the field. When they were signalled to slow, Villeneuve obeyed and Pironi passed him. Villeneuve re-took the lead but when the 'slow' signal was shown again Pironi did the same thing! He stayed in front of an incandescent Villeneuve to the flag. Sadly it was Villeneuve's last race; he was killed during practice for the next round in Belgium.

In the autumn of 1983 sports cars came back to Imola to race over 1,000km in a round of the European Sports Car Championship. It was a thin field and an equally thin crowd which saw a rare Lancia win. The distance was 1,000km again in 1984, this time for the World Endurance Championship. It was a bad day for the *tricolore*. Porsches took the first eight places, the best Lancia finishing ninth.

NELSON PIQUET

NELSON PIQUET followed the same route as many Brazilian drivers. He came to England from South America to seek his fortune in Formula 3, prospering by becoming the class champion. Bernie Ecclestone, then running the Brabham F1 team, spotted his talent and recruited Piquet in 1979. Nelson coped with the uncompetitive Brabham-Alfa Romeo for a season. Then, in 1980, he was given a Brabham with Cosworth DFV power. This set him on the road to success.

When the Grand Prix circus came to Imola for the 1980 Italian GP, Piquet knew the track, having raced a Formula 3 Ralt there in 1977. Nelson was third away from the start. Profiting from his experience of Imola, in two laps he nipped past the Renaults of Arnoux and Jabouille. Once in front, he pulled away from the field and took the flag nearly half a minute ahead. His third Championship win of the season, it helped make him runner-up for the title.

The San Marino Grand Prix became a full Championship round in 1981, a season whose early months had been marred by squabbles between the teams and FISA about the eligibility of skirts, ground effects and ride heights. The Imola race was run in an atmosphere of acrimony.

In wet conditions Piquet began cautiously in eighth place. Having made the right choice of tyres, he began to move up the list as others stopped to change rubber or indulge in minor accidents. After 20 laps he was up to second and went into the lead 13 laps before the finish. In the conditions it was a mature, considered drive. It paid off. Piquet ended the season as Champion, repeating the success in 1983.

Though Piquet never achieved the same success at Imola, he came close in 1986. Having moved to Williams he led the race, but found his turbo-boosted fuel consumption was excessive. Obliged to back off, he lost the lead. Prost, who headed the field in a McLaren, had to slow on his last lap with lack of fuel. Piquet was just too far behind to profit, losing the race by seven seconds.

Piquet won another Championship in 1987 and picked up a third place at Imola in 1988. Some of the fire had gone from his racing and he retired at the end of 1991. Critics cavilled that Piquet was not the most thrusting of drivers, but as he showed at Imola in 1981 he raced with his head as well as his heart.

In the early laps of the 1990 San Marino Grand Prix, Riccardo Patrese's Williams FW13 leads Jean Alesi's Tyrell 019 while the Ferraris of Nigel Mansell and Alain Prost are in pursuit. Patrese holds off the field to win.

161

An aerial view depicts the Imola circuit in 1990.

Far right: **Races at Imola always arouse the passions of the pro-Ferrari tifosi.**

Nigel Mansell acknowledges the flag as he wins the 1992 San Marino Grand Prix in a Williams FW14B. This is one of the wins which secures his World Championship.

One hundred thousand spectators watched the 1983 Grand Prix. René Arnoux put his Ferrari on the front row of the grid, so local hopes were high. They weren't disappointed. After a fierce battle with Prost's Renault and Ricardo Patrese's Brabham, Ferrari's Patrick Tambay came home to win. Arnoux was third, nursing an ailing engine. It was close as Tambay ran out of fuel on the slowing-down lap.

The turbo engines which now dominated Formula 1 were thirsty. In the 1984 Grand Prix all the front runners except Prost had to ease off in the closing laps and cruise to make the finish. Prost sailed on. With the help of Porsche, which had built its TAG-Turbo V6, the McLaren team did their sums and he took the flag.

Imola seemed to produce drama both on and off the track. The 1985 F1 race saw the new star Ayrton Senna lead all the way until, with three laps to go, his Lotus ran out of fuel. The lead was inherited by Swede Stefan Johansson's Ferrari. Half a lap later that too had an empty tank. Prost kept his McLaren going to take the flag, running out of fuel just after the line. He seemed to be the winner but his car was disqualified for scaling three kilograms under the limit. The winner was Elio de Angelis, whose Lotus had never occupied first spot during the race proper.

Fuel consumption continued to be the ruling factor at Imola. Piquet's Williams led in 1986 until his consumption dictated a reduced speed. This let the McLarens of Prost and Rosberg go by. Piquet's pit did sums and speeded him up again. He closed on the McLarens, then with two laps to go Rosberg ran out of fuel. On the last lap Prost almost spluttered to a halt. When he swung his McLaren from side to side its pumps picked up enough fuel to take him to the flag, just in front of a charging Piquet.

Nigel Mansell took the flag in 1987, and Senna had a runaway win in 1988, when the circuit was renamed Autodromo Enzo e Dino Ferrari following the death of the legendary Enzo. There was drama again in 1989. After three laps Gerhard Berger's Ferrari hit a retaining wall and burst into flames. When the race was stopped the marshals pulled him out, only slightly burned. After the restart Senna had another runaway win.

The brilliant Senna won again in 1990, taking the Championship at the end of the season. This set a pattern, for the winners in the three subsequent years, Mansell, Prost and Michael Schumacher, went on to become Champion. It was Schumacher who took the flag, mourning Senna, in 1994. His relentless pursuit of the Brazilian in the early laps ended when Senna crashed with fatal consequences.

For 1995, perhaps in an over-reaction to the two deaths,

the circuit was changed with the installation of more chicanes. The drivers didn't like the changes, which increased the lap distance to 3.06 miles (4.93km). They said they broke up the fluency of the corners. Damon Hill scored on the revised circuit in 1995 and 1996. He too went on to the Championship in 1996. Scotsman David Coulthard won a canny race in 1998 when his engine was overheating. He led from flag to flag, just maintaining enough speed to keep Schumacher at bay.

For six years from 1999 to 2004 the San Marino GP became a Schumacher benefit. It was Michael and Ferrari every time save in 2001 when younger brother Ralf scored his first Championship race win with a Williams. The race had become the Gran Premio Warsteiner di San Marino in recognition of its brewer sponsor.

Spaniard Fernando Alonso, the new kid on the block, took the 2005 race, now with another brewery sponsor, Fosters. He held off Michael Schumacher, who chased all the way after delays at pit stops and only failed to catch up by a mere fifth of a second at the finish. Roles were reversed in 2006, Schumacher's last season before his 2010 return, when despite deteriorating tyres he kept Alonso at bay.

Formula 1's ringmasters had been complaining that Imola, albeit still offering rural charm, was falling behind the brave new world that was emerging. It compared poorly with the glitzy new purpose-built circuits, especially in the Third World. The San Marino race was dropped from the Championship calendar for 2007 and has not been reinstated since.

In 2009 the circuit had a major revamp. Italian national racing returned and a Formula 2 race was run in September 2009. The declared aim was to secure the return of the World Championship. In its relatively short life Imola has seen more drama than most circuits, while its spectators have a fire and passion only matched at rival Monza.

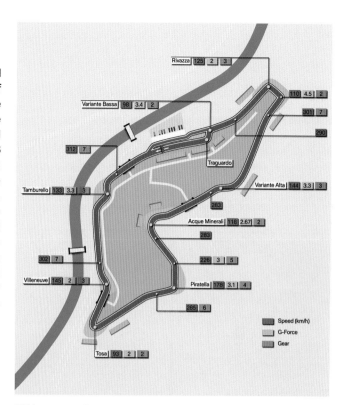

Track plan of Imola in 2002, showing speed, gears and G-force on selected areas of the track.

Michael Schumacher's F310 Ferrari passes the massed ranks of the tifosi during the 1996 San Marino Grand Prix. He finishes second, 16 seconds behind Damon Hill.

The Ferrari F93A of Jean Alesi takes the Acque Minerale turn in the 1993 San Marino Grand Prix.

Alessandro Zanardi drives a Williams FW 21 in the 1999 San Marino Grand Prix. He had a bad day, finishing last.

Right: At the start of the 2003 San Marino Grand Prix, Michael Schumacher leads the field in his Ferrari F2002/3GA, followed by his team-mate Rubens Barichello. Ralf Schumacher's Williams FW25 takes a wider line.

Michael Schumacher is on his way to win the 2003 San Marino Grand Prix in a Ferrari F2002/3GA, designated to honour recently deceased Fiat chief Giovanni Agnelli.

A high angle shows the crowded Imola pits and paddock in 2006.

CHAPTER 20

Hungaroring

Two views show Tazio Nuvolari's 8C35 Alfa Romeo at the primitive pits during practice for the 1936 Hungarian Grand Prix (Magyar Nagydíj). Nuvolari drives a remarkable race, beating the more powerful German teams.

PERSONAL ambition and commercial aspirations combined to create the Hungaroring. In the early 1980s Bernie Ecclestone, the boss of the Formula One Constructors' Association, went in search of new venues. He realised that behind the Iron Curtain, still splitting Europe, were potentially lucrative sites for World Championship races.

Despite the suffocating Communist ideology, countless motor-racing enthusiasts in Eastern Europe wanted to witness the drama and excitement of Formula 1. Ecclestone looked around the Eastern Bloc countries. Hoping for a race in Russia he began negotiations with the Soviet government, but the talks bogged down in endless bureaucracy. Eventually Ecclestone decided that Hungary looked the best prospect for the development he wanted.

Back in 1936 Hungary had hosted a Grand Prix, the Magyar Nagydíj, in Budapest. Held in the Nepliget Park in the

centre of the city, it drew the Mercedes-Benz and Auto Union teams. Its serpentine 3.1-mile (4.9-km) road circuit was expected to produce a German walk-over, but Tazio Nuvolari had other ideas. In an underpowered and outclassed 8C 35 Alfa Romeo he out-drove the German aces and scored a notable win.

No more significant motor racing took place in Hungary until the 1960s. Hungarian leader János Kádár, taking note of the national uprising against the occupying Soviet forces in 1956, began introducing a more liberal regime. Some motor racing was allowed to return, again on the Nepliget circuit. Rounds of the European Touring Car Championship, together with Formula 3 and Formula Vee races, were promoted.

Bernie Ecclestone first thought of bringing the Championship circus to Nepliget Park, visualising a circuit on the lines of Monaco. He began negotiations with the Hungarian government via an intermediary, Tamés Rohanyi. These were protracted, until in 1983 he received indications that omens were favourable. However, the Hungarian authorities decided that a permanent purpose-built circuit would have more value and utility. A site was chosen at Mogyoród about 12 miles (19km) north-east of Budapest. It was a green-field site, a natural amphitheatre in open country adjacent to an Autoroute.

A pact between FOCA and the Hungarian authorities was signed in London in September 1985. A month later construction of the circuit began. Eight months later the Hungaroring was ready, a tight circuit with 16 corners in its 2.5-mile (4.0-km) lap. After a motorcycle meeting was held in March of 1986, in August the Formula 1 circus rolled into town. It was the second Magyar Nagydij, but this time it was the first Hungarian World Championship round.

The drivers had divided views on the newcomer. Among those who liked its tight curves was Ayrton Senna, still climbing toward his first Championship. Others found it hard work, with all agreeing that it offered few places for overtaking. Martin Brundle called it 'a street circuit without houses'.

Senna held pole position for this 1986 debut event in his Lotus and led for two thirds of the race, but then slowed. Nelson Piquet went past to score a win for Williams. The race should have been over 77 laps, but with a lap to go the regulation two hours were up and the cars were flagged to a finish.

A year later Hungary should have been Nigel Mansell's race. Misfortune seemed to stalk him during the 1980s. For several seasons the Championship was almost in his grasp when fate intervened. At the Hungaroring he dominated with a win seeming certain when a wheel nut came off his Williams. With six laps to go he sat impotent beside the track to see Piquet take the flag, going on to become Champion at the end of the season. The lost Magyar points might have made the difference for Mansell.

When the Grand Prix drivers came to the Hungaroring they had a problem not encountered at other circuits of the 1980s. With the track used for only one major event a year, ample dust from the surrounding sandy soil was spread on its surface. At other venues regular racing kept the track surface clear.

The savage bitter years of the Prost-Senna feud had begun. Though both men were masterful, they were poles apart in temperament. That both were in the McLaren team in 1988 further heightened that season's tension. Prost made a slow start but came through to hound the leading Senna. After he took the lead, Senna snatched it back. Trying to outbrake Senna, Prost 'flatted' a tyre. This made the difference. Senna led him across the line by a mere 0.4sec.

The monolithic Soviet empire was beginning to show cracks. With fewer fetters from the east, Hungary began to seek greater freedom and more open contact with the West. In 1989

Hungary declared itself a democratic republic. The border guards departed and the frontier with Austria was opened. After 1987 the Austrian Grand Prix had been abandoned, so deprived Austrian fans flocked to the Hungaroring, making it their surrogate home circuit. Until 1989 the Hungaroring had been a semi-political East-European totem. Now it became a proper commercial venture.

Cars were getting quicker and one of the corners was eased off, which made for a slighter faster lap, so in 1989 the race distance was lengthened to 77 laps. The Austrian fans went home with something to remember. The Prost-Senna feud still raged within the McLaren team, but Prost's car was off form. It looked like an easy cruise to victory for Senna, but Mansell had other ideas. Mansell outwitted Senna as they lapped a back marker and once in front, the Birmingham driver stayed there to win.

The frustrations of passing on the Hungaroring were emphasised for Senna in 1990. Belgian Thierry Boutsen's Williams led all the way. After Senna was held up by a minor bump with a back marker, he caught Boutsen but couldn't not find a way through, despite having the faster car. Senna made up for this frustration by walking away with the race for the next two years.

Budapest was a long journey for British fans, but those who made the trip had full compensation in 1993. Damon Hill, son of the legendary Graham, scored his first Championship win in a Williams. He did it again in 1995. Another son of a great driver, Jacques Villeneuve, pulled off victories in the next two years.

During the last 15 years the Hungaroring has drawn a big contingent of spectators from Finland. In 1998 they had every reason to come. The Formula 1 circus came to Hungary with one of their countrymen, Mika Häkkinen, leading the Championship and on his way to the title. He was outwitted that day by Michael Schumacher, aided by the brilliant management of Ferrari boss Ross Brawn. With carefully timed stops, Schumacher won and Häkkinen came sixth.

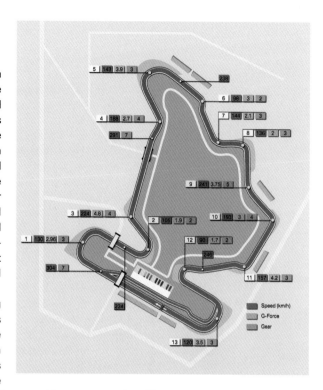

Circuit diagram showing typical speeds, G-force and gears as used in F1, 2002.

After the 1998 race the FIA fined the Hungarian organisers $1 million for a crowd invasion of the track, prohibited by its rules. Three-quarters of the penalty was suspended pending good crowd behaviour in the next two years. Luckily the crowd behaved itself, so the funds stayed in Budapest.

The Finnish fans could have shown their delight by a track invasion after the races of 1999 and 2000 when Häkkinen took the honours both years in a McLaren-Mercedes. Next the golden years of Michael Schumacher and Ferrari came to magnificent fruition. Schumacher took the Magyar Nagydij in 2001 and his team-mate, Brazil's Rubens Barrichello, scored in 2002.

A new generation was starting to emerge. At the forefront was scintillating young Spaniard Fernando Alonso, driving for a revitalised Renault team. Through the 2003 season his first win was anticipated. It came at the Hungaroring when he led from flag to flag. He won on a revised circuit with a short extension to the main straight and a sharpened corner leading to it. The changes were intended to make passing easier and more frequent, but the difference was barely noticeable.

When Briton Jenson Button graduated to Formula 1 in 2001, a brilliant future was predicted. After he was kicked out of the Renault team by boss Flavio Briatore at the end of 2002, however, to make way for the emerging Alonso, Button struggled. He began to accrue a 'no-hoper' reputation in the Championship circus.

To Button's huge relief — and that of his many admirers — he showed he could be a winner by scoring his first Championship victory in the 2006 Magyar Nagydij. His win was not an easy one as he picked his way up the race order from 14th place on the opening lap, taking advantage of his smooth car control in the first wet race held on the Hungaroring. The win was some recompense for Button's hitherto unsuccessful Honda team.

The McLaren-Mercedes team must have had a feeling of déjà vu in 2007 when the bitter rivalry of the Prost-Senna years was echoed by the relationship between nominal team leader Fernando Alonso and his upstart rival, Formula 1 rookie Lewis Hamilton. Alonso had been tipped to win the Championship, but bursting onto the scene at the beginning of the season, Hamilton showed he was as fast as the best of his rivals — which no longer included Michael Schumacher.

By the time the teams arrived in Hungary, Alonso was deeply unhappy. Hamilton was showing the form and taking the wins that could frustrate the Spaniard's expectations. With a good grid position essential on a circuit where passing is difficult, qualifying didn't go well. Sitting in the pit lane ahead of Hamilton, Alonso didn't move when the cars were released,

AYRTON SENNA

BRAZIL'S Ayrton Senna had a remarkable empathy with the Hungaroring. He competed in nine Championship races on the circuit and either won or finished second in every race bar his last appearance.

In the inaugural race in 1986 he came second in a Lotus-Renault and repeated this the following year. In 1988 Senna, now in a McLaren-Honda, took an immediate lead. Alain Prost, nominally his McLaren team-mate but in fact his bitter rival, made a slow start but gradually reeled Senna in. He took a chance when the pair lapped a back marker, seizing the lead but then running wide; Senna dashed back in front. Prost had flatted a tyre in his abortive overtake, but was only half a second behind when the pair took the flag.

The audacious Senna received some of his own medicine in 1989. After tracking Riccardo Patrese's Williams for 50 laps, he took the lead when Patrese pulled off. Behind this pair Mansell had come through in his Ferrari and closed on Senna. Lapping a back marker, Mansell forced his way through, leaving no room for Senna who had to settle for second place.

Another second place was registered in 1990 when Belgian Thierry Boutsen led all the way. Senna caught up with him after a slow start. He might have taken the lead, but the Hungarian circuit's constraints on passing and a minor collision with the Benetton of Alessandro Nannini left Senna a mere third of a second behind as they crossed the line.

It was a different story in 1991 when a masterful Ayrton Senna led all the way, dictating the pace of the race in his McLaren. Mansell closed up at the end but Senna held all the cards. It came a little harder in 1992 when Senna had to trail Patrese's Williams until its Renault engine gave up at two-thirds distance. Ayrton then took the lead, pulling away from the rest to score another convincing win that contributed points to his 1991 World Championship.

Spectators last saw Senna at the Hungaroring in 1993, when he suffered his only retirement at the circuit. His McLaren cried enough after 18 laps when he was in a challenging second place.

It is never possible to say a driver was 'the greatest of all time'. Criteria change in different eras. But Senna was by all odds the greatest of his generation.

Ivan Capelli crests a rise in his Ferrari F92A during the 1992 Grand Prix. He finishes sixth.

Michael Schumacher is still on his way to the top in the 1993 Grand Prix. In a Benetton B192 he tracks the Ferrari F93A of Gerhard Berger, followed by his Benetton team-mate Riccardo Patrese.

Below: **Michael Schumacher is acclaimed by the Ferrari fans as he wins the 1998 Grand Prix after one of his greatest drives.**

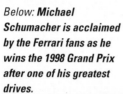

Michael Schumacher's Ferrari F1-2000 gets a nose ahead of David Coulthard's McLaren-Mercedes MP4/15 at the first corner of the 2000 Grand Prix. Mika Häkkinen, the race winner, follows the Ferrari. Two corners later Coulthard is eliminated in a multi-car collision.

Ralf Schumacher exits the pits in his Williams-BMW FW22 during the 2000 Grand Prix. He finishes fifth.

Rubens Barichello takes the race ahead of his team leader Michael Schumacher in a Ferrari 1-2 at the 2002 Hungarian Grand Prix.

170

Mark Webber races his Williams-Cosworth FW28 past a water fun fair during practice for the 2006 Grand Prix. He spins off on the first lap.

keeping Hamilton from getting onto the circuit soon enough to improve his previous time.

Alonso and the McLaren team were penalised, the Spanish driver moved back five places on the grid. Hamilton had his revenge in the sweetest way, leading from flag to flag. At the podium ceremony after the race the penalty was evident as no trophy was presented to McLaren as the winning constructor. It received no Constructors' points for its victory.

The Hungaroring seems to galvanise not only Finland's fans but its drivers as well. The 'Ice Man', Kimi Räikkönen, had taken the 2005 race for McLaren-Mercedes after good pit-stop timing and strategy put him in front of Schumacher's Ferrari. At the end of 2007 Alonso left McLaren amid much bitterness and was replaced by Finland's Heikki Kovalainen.

In the early laps of the 2008 race Felipe Massa's Ferrari led Hamilton, then the young Briton's hopes were dashed by a puncture which put him at the back of the field. Kovalainen now pursued Massa. Three laps from the finish Massa's engine burst in a cloud of smoke and the Finn took the flag for his first Championship win. The Finnish flags waved with redoubled vigour as Räikkönen, now in a Ferrari, came through to third.

Qualifying for the 2009 Magyar Nagydij brought distressing drama. Dislodged from the rear suspension of the Brawn of Rubens Barichello, a coil spring bounced off the track and struck Felipe Massa, following in his Ferrari. The dazed Massa's car went off the track and hit the bank. For a while there were fears for Massa's career after his left eye was damaged, but he recovered.

Hamilton, who won the 2008 Championship, was having a dismal season in 2009 with his McLaren well off the pace. However the Hungaroring saw a huge upturn in his fortunes. After Alonso lost a wheel from his Renault, Hamilton went on to take his first win of the season. This was a first race win for a car fitted with KERS, the regenerative system which gave an occasional extra short burst of power using energy recouped while braking. It was used by Hamilton to good effect during the race.

Although not used as much as most purpose-built circuits, the Hungaroring has hosted rounds of the German touring car championship and the FIA GT Championship. In its relatively short life it has been the stage for huge drama. The trees planted when it was opened are maturing, giving it a pleasant rural aspect. The first circuit to bring Formula 1 to a wider audience, the Hungaroring was the forerunner of the swathe of new tracks which have changed the face of top-class racing.

Nico Rosberg (Williams-Toyota FW31) leads the McLaren MP4/24 of Heikki Kovalainen through a chicane in the early laps of the 2009 Grand Prix. Rosberg finishes fourth and Kovalainen fifth.

Lewis Hamilton has a change of fortune in the 2009 Grand Prix. After a dismal season he scores his first win there with his McLaren MP4/24.

BIBLIOGRAPHY

Boddy, William, *Montlhéry* (Cassel 1961)

——, *The Motor Sport Book of Donington* (Grenville Publishing 1973)

——, *Brooklands, The Complete Motor Racing History* (MRP 2001)

Bradley W.F., *Targa Florio* (G.T. Foulis & Co 1956)

Carli, Emanuele Alberto, *Settant'Anni di Gare Automobilistiche in Italia* (AC d'Italia Editrice dell Automobile 1967)

Hodges, David, *The Le Mans 24-Hour Race* (Temple Press 1963)

——, *The Monaco Grand Prix* (Temple Press 1964)

——, *The French Grand Prix* (Temple Press 1967)

Kupelian, Yvette and Sirtaine, Jacques, *Soixante Ans de Competition Automobile en Belgique 1896-1956* (Kupelian & Du Bock 2001)

Mathieson,T.A.S.O., *Grand Prix Racing 1906-1914* (Connaisseur Automobile 1964)

Moity, Christian, Teissedre, Jean-Marc,and Bienvenue, Alain, *24 Heures du Mans 1923-1992* (Editions d'Art J.P. Barthelemy 1992)

Monza, *Official Year Books 1960-64* (SIAS 1961-65)

Nixon, Chris, *Racing the Silver Arrows* (Osprey 1986)

Parker, Chas, *Brands Hatch* (Haynes 2008)

Pascal, Dominique, *Les Grandes Heures de Montlhéry* (ETAI 2004)

Posthumus, Cyril, *The German Grand Prix* (Temple Press 1966)

Sheldon, Paul, *A Record of Grand Prix & Voiturette Racing, Vols 1-13* (St Leonards Press 1987-2002)

Williams, Richard, *The Last Road Race, The 1957 Pescara Grand Prix* (Weidenfeld & Nicholson 2004)

Wimpffen, Janos, *Time and Two Seats* (Motor Sports Research Group 1999)

The Autocar
Autosport
The Motor
Motor Racing
Motor Sport
Speed